Information and Institutions of Government Accountability

Len Cook and Robert Hughes

Information and Institutions of Government Accountability
by Len Cook and Robert Hughes

Published in 2018 by Hughes Books an imprint of Hughes Consulting Limited
NZBN 9429038579288

www.HughesBooks.Info

Alpha Edition

ISBN 978-0-473-43893-7 (Paperback)
ISBN 978-0-473-43894-4 (ePub)

A catalogue record of this book is available from the National Library of New Zealand Te Puna Matauranga o Aotearoa.

Image credits

The authors and publisher would like to thank David Low/ Solo Syndication for permission to reproduce the cartoons of David Low (1891–1963), images supplied by the British Cartoon Archive, University of Kent:

Hmm…Maybe there's something in these slogans, originally published in 4 July 1947.

I know what it needs, boss! Foundations!, originally published in 19 July 1943.

Open wide, please. I'm afraid this might hurt a little, originally published in 9 December 1948.

Phew! that's a nasty leak. Thank goodness it's not at our end of the boat, originally published in 24 March 1932.

Speedway model, originally published in 5 September 1938.

The Government is about to turn the corner, originally published in 2 June 1930.

The little thing that puzzles him, originally published in 13 September 1928.

There, I knew we'd forgotten something! We forgot to control the pig, originally published in 10 January 1935.

Contents

"The task of the statistician is to study humanity and report when things are not as they should be."[1]

Preface

This book has been prepared by two experienced practitioners with a wide range of expearience in the place of information in the public sector, community and business, and its implications for the value that government brings. The book distils a small number of substantive themes and commonalities out of a wide and varied range of situations and events from both contemporary issues and the recent past. It is practical situations and experiences that inform the analysis of this book, which is not a review of theory but is naturally shaped by the fields of learning of each of the authors.

Properly holding government to account is a challenge to the expediency of political life and the ineffective shaping and framing of the future that results.

By not properly holding government to account, executive government itself functions less transparently and effectively so that policies are less relevant to current and future needs than they could be.

This book is written for people involved in government, and those who deal with public services, and civil society. Most especially civil society needs to be kept aware of the uncertainty inherent in all information that is the knowledge base for policy and service delivery, and that deliberately avoiding this obligation is tampering with the evidence.

This study is not a static piece of work, but the distillation of thinking about information that needs to underpin responses to big data, public sector management, and government accountability. It will be updated periodically, as systems advance, situations evolve, and the need for enriched thinking about government accountability becomes more pronounced.

We selected the cartoons of Sir David Low for the chapters in this book because of their enduring relevance to holding government to account. That they relate to another country and another time reminds us that this is an eternal issue where continual dissatisfaction leads to periodic leaps of faith in some new mechanism which will itself be later found wanting.

We would like to acknowledge the comments made by a number of people to early drafts of this text, and to the anonymous reader who provided us with thoughtful feedback.

Len Cook and Robert Hughes

Introduction

Government has a vital role in ensuring the availability of a wide range of appropriate information to its citizens. Two reasons for this are: to enable the state to do its job by building up the capacity to deliver the functions of state; and to understand, anticipate and respond to change (including unexpected events) in social, economic and environmental conditions. In doing this, it also needs to ensure that citizens can hold government to account for its actions.

It is through a multitude of ways for the systematic accumulation of appropriate information that government builds the collective knowledge essential to anticipate or to react so as to make progress in the face of change. When obtained in a manner that retains the trust of citizens, trustworthy information is a counterweight to ineffective policies, lightly given populist promises, undue influence of lobby groups and corrupt practices, along with avoidable failures. As well as making transparent the speculation that is an ever-present and necessary component of public and private decisions, trustworthy information is required to enable citizens to intelligently place and reject trust in public provided, regulated or funded services, and in this way to hold government to account through democratic processes.

Public confidence in the systems of government, and their capacity to maintain functions is fundamental to ensuring that the integrity of the state is sustained. Reliance on the systems of government needs to be above the Government of the day and regardless of agreement with their policies or trust in the people who form the elected executive of the time. One important reason for this is that particular public sector institutions themselves can dramatically fail the people they are supposed to assist. There are many examples from New Zealand's history of outcomes which point to misplaced trust in what proved to be poorly designed or poorly administered functions of government. Examples range from institutional child abuse and a long-running inability to effectively address child protection, to ineffectual financial and safety deregulation where past failure has been borne by innocent individuals. Systemic failures of these types whose impact persists for long periods of time have been more likely where there is reduced inclination to hold the state to account by independent oversight.

These are important issues today. Diminishing public confidence is seen in declining turnout at elections, open distrust of politicians, and rising visibility of the personal costs to citizens associated with poor value-for-money from government policies. Distrust can result in citizens making poor decisions regarding the functions of government and in their use of public provided, regulated or funded services. The consequence is that where government is seen to have become less effective or not warrant the trust of citizens, then the levers familiar to politicians and policy-makers lose effectiveness. One response by government aimed at strengthening public confidence has been the growth in oversight bodies, such as the Independent Police Complaints Authority, the Inspector-General of Intelligence and Security, the Health and Disability Authority, and WorkSafe New Zealand. In extreme cases, loss of trust is manifested in social unrest. New Zealand has a long history of public demonstrations when the state loses touch with communities.

We make the case that the counterweight to the Government's ability to drive change, is the provision in appropriate ways and forms of trustworthy information that give citizens confidence that they can hold government to account. The key test of appropriate information is whether government enables evidence that genuinely reflects the conditions faced by the concerned citizen and their communities of interest. Through such evidence, citizens can see the status of the capacity to accommodate their concerns, and to hold government to account for the failure to address them. For example, the introduction in 1996 of regular surveys of disability along with the five yearly Censuses of Population after vigorous challenge by the disability community, heralded a systematic way in which that community could engage with the state to improve their wellbeing.

To hold government to account is to provide the ability of any citizen and their communities of interest to access information that: gives line-of-sight into their particular circumstances; and which shows that the relevant functions of government are trustworthy. This ability to access information is not time bound, nor does it require foresight on the collection of information (although this helps). The ability to hold to account requires the capacity to challenge government. This is illustrated by the work that was undertaken to reconstruct the evidence to redress Treaty of Waitangi grievances. Limited records were kept of the impact of the actions of the government of the day, and research techniques developed by historians were used to create an evidence base. This evidence also showed that for these communities, at the time, the functions of government were untrustworthy.

This book is about the information that government needs to provide to its citizens, and the obligations that bring this about. The book explains the role played by information in government, and the drivers, obligations and levers operating on and available to government. It also examines the consequences of inappropriate response to these drivers, poor choice of levers, loose obligations and inadequate information on the effectiveness and cost of government. The mechanisms to hold government to account cover information on policies, information to build the capacity of society, economy and environment, information to assess operational performance, and information produced to enable people to intelligently place or refuse trust in public provided or funded services.

In setting out a framework for the place of information in government we provide an approach to understanding public sector management that recognises the intensity of pressures that will be faced in the coming decades, and the uncertainties associated with them. We explore what government needs to take account of, so as to enhance understanding of what things get done and how. The organisation of public institutions, their roles, inter-relationships, knowledge management and accountability need to give government the capacity to meet its obligations to citizens in a constitutionally sound manner. The central issue is: how do citizens have instituted the information systems needed to do this?

"PHEW! THAT'S A NASTY LEAK. THANK GOODNESS ITS NOT AT OUR END OF THE BOAT."

Chapter 1

The New Zealand form of the Westminster constitutional system

Changes in groups accommodated by constitutional arrangements

The form of the Westminster system of government operated in
New Zealand has proven to be flexible to changes in the communities
of interest accommodated by constitutional arrangements and how
these groups participate in government. As examples of this, over the
last three decades, Governments have shifted their stance on how
they accommodate Māori, as well as ethnic communities and recent
migrant groups. Governments have also recognised distinct rights for
those whose disability or sexual orientation previously diminished them
as citizens in statute, convention or accountability processes. There is

a much-strengthened recognition of the Treaty of Waitangi and giving effect to its obligations. The state of marriage is no longer a key basis for determining household entitlements when dealing with the public sector.

These changed accommodations have been wide-ranging. Authority has been granted to the Auckland and Christchurch regional bodies for the making and implementing of environmental and transportation policies. Obligations on citizens through business practice have been created by international treaties[2]. Along with the adoption of constitutional arrangements to recognise communities of significance previously unrecognised by public administration, at the policy level citizen participation has moved from representative democracy towards a form of participative democracy with fragmented interest groups having the capacity for an effective veto power.

The eclectic nature of the constitutional arrangements that are in place means that there is no specific common process or certainty of a proper change process as arrangements are challenged. Cabinet generally directs and controls policy and is responsible to Parliament. It also has the dominant influence over law making. Cabinet itself exists purely by constitutional convention as it has no formal statutory basis and is not established by any legislative act. A constitution is usually thought of as a steadying influence on government decision-making, albeit one able to slowly evolve. However, in New Zealand conventions and statutes can develop quickly, and sometimes unwittingly. Despite the rule of law and the expected impartiality of the public service, there appears to be a growing degree of Ministerial direction at an operational level, beyond the expected policy leadership. This is exemplified by the creation of special ministerial roles for the Christchurch rebuild, and the 2013 Rugby World Cup.

This propensity of the constitutional arrangements to react and respond to the social and economic context is a major benefit of the trust of the electorate in the New Zealand form of the Westminster system. Trustworthiness in government is underpinned by institutional and statutory disciplines to support the accountability of the House of Representatives and hence government. Electorate boundaries are reset every five years through rules and processes that prevent the gerrymandering seen in many respected democracies. A strong feature of this implementation is the capacity of franchised citizens to vote to bring about change in elected representatives and the executive every three years.

Members of Parliament (MPs) are elected to a single house legislative assembly under a Mixed Member Proportional (MMP) voting system. The MMP voting system is the electoral process in which voters have two votes, one for a local candidate and the other for a party. The party vote determines the proportion of the total number of members a party has in the House of Representatives. Where this proportion is greater than the number of elected members, then the balance is drawn from the party list selected by the party. There are currently 64 general electorate seats and seven Māori electorate seats. 49 seats are for list candidates (this number can vary according to the total voting proportions, as seen in the House of Representatives of 2015-2017 where there were 121 MPs).

The House of Representatives, the Governor-General, the Judiciary and the Chief Justice, Controller and Auditor-General (C&AG), and Treasury are fundamental to the integrity of constitutional government in New Zealand, as well as those institutions which have long played a key part in trust in government, such as the State Services Commissioner, Solicitor-General, Commissioner of Police, Chief Electoral Officer, Government Statistician, Chief of the Defence Force, and the Ombudsman. The functions of these institutions do not change when the constitution is adjusted; their world view of the present and future is tempered by their inheritance of role, place, convention and accumulated case law. These institutions and roles are a legacy from past governments to the present, and unlike many other public institutions, the role, function and practices of these particular bodies are well established in statute.

But this is an imperfect relationship between the citizen and the Government of the day. Despite the integrity of electoral processes, the way in which candidates, political parties and other interest groups behave during the lead up to elections risks creating distrust in electoral processes. An example of this behaviour is the limited capacity of voters to withdraw support on specific matters in a party's manifesto. While the share of votes a political party attracts may on balance reflect their relative attractiveness to the electorate, this does not mean that all policies are supported equally. Allied to this, the framing of issues by interest groups to fit public sentiment can detract from the significant issues, including questions of the trustworthiness of government decisions.

Ministerial appointments are drawn from MPs in the governing parties, some of whom may be list MPs. The executive is held to account by opposition MPs and Select Committees. The dominance of the House of Representatives by the executive is regarded by some as diminishing the authority of the legislature as a distinct entity with distinct roles and behaviours. The Speaker of Parliament retains connections with the dominant political party and is not totally independent. One by-product of MMP is that nearly half of the MPs are selected not by an electorate but by the elites of political parties, which have evolved in most cases to be dominated by the Parliamentarians themselves. A significant share of backbench members of the parties that form the executive at any time are beholden to their political party leaders in two ways, both as 'Ministers in waiting', and always needing confirmation of their place on the party list at later elections. Government backbench members rarely play a part in Parliament in holding Ministers to account, regardless of which political parties lead the executive.

Consistently strong challenge on Ministers from outside government is problematic. There are few means of challenge based on well researched and structured interactions in Parliament, and that from the media is varied and inconsistent, and can be frustrated by delays in accessing official information. Independently funded research centres are all small.

Exacerbating this, the tendency by Ministers to feel the need to provide instant answers flies in the face of the thoughtful context within which public policy is best developed, evaluated, decided on, and then put in place. Personality issues and flaws make better reading as human interest stories in media in comparison to dry policy analysis – not that following a thoughtful process to formulate public policy is without its limitations.

It is also an imperfect relationship because when there is information on the performance of government available for the knowledgeable professionals with resources to analyse it, the information is usually not particularly effective at conveying the true state of the nation to the public. For example, governments extol their success as economic managers by using macroscopic measures such as improved Gross Domestic Product. Such measures are meaningless to a school leaver in Manurewa trying to enter the workforce, whose friends face similar challenges. Successful economic management by the government for the school leaver is gainful employment for them and their community – this is the information that would be useful to them. Although it is likely that services will fail citizens in some way, few measures have been developed by government agencies that recognise the value to its citizens in monitoring service failures.

In government provided information there is a high focus on short-term cost efficiency, which is not complemented by concerns of usefulness or effectiveness. This points to a command and control management model, rather than interconnected networks and a drive for continuous improvement. This leads to a lack of empowerment of the electorate to place and refuse trust in the services and processes of government. Perversely, the increased responsiveness of government to accommodate new communities of interest, has been accompanied by a diminution in the accountability of the executive to citizens.

Limited adaptivity of the public administration as a system

Government makes things happen using systems, processes and procedures that perform not only the functions of government, but also those of business, community organisations, local government and global enterprises. The distinctness of any government system is a result of particular areas of specialist expertise, investment form, statutory characteristics or constitutional place. For example, the authority to tax has been retained as the sole responsibility of central government, and tax gathering is almost always done by public servants. In such cases, government not only enables understanding of an area of public life, it is also the key actor in enabling things to happen. There are government processes which reflect a smaller interest in control, such as various areas of social welfare support that are contracted out for delivery by the private and not-for-profit sectors.

The public sector consists of a variety of entities each charged, since the inception of the Public Finance Act 1989, to deliver or have delivered specified results in the outputs and outcomes set out in performance agreements between responsible Ministers and the chief executives of public sector entities. These outputs, outcomes and the associated funding are agreed through a formal process culminating in the appropriation of funds by Parliament in the annual budget. Policy development along with that of funder generally involves the public sector, but other critical elements such as standard setter, service network platform manager or direct provider that make up programme management, may not involve the public sector (e.g. School Trustees Association).

Monitoring and evaluation of performance of the public sector in delivering the specified outputs for the appropriated funds takes place through the financial management process and the supporting evaluation of the performance of chief executives. Monitoring performance in delivering the specified outputs is done with a variety of sources of information. This includes operational information collected by entities, and in some cases official statistics are used. The State Services Commissioner undertakes the evaluation of chief executives and the State Sector Act 1988 extends the scope of reviews to enable evaluation of the value-for-money delivered. There are two additional features of this process, provided in the Public Finance Act 1989. First is the requirement for the Government to provide comprehensive financial information; and the second, is that the Government must specify its intentions for fiscal management beyond the next 12 months. Every four years the Treasury is required to publish a Statement on the Long-term Fiscal Position, and an Investment Statement.

These mechanisms are intended to provide a high degree of visibility on planned expenditure, but the systematised re-assessment of existing policies and programmes is rare, and weak where it takes place[3]. There is a false sense of comfort where the annual budget estimates continually fail to recognise the inherent unpredictability of particular spending obligations, and the variability of small entities and communities. They also provide a false sense of comfort in the capacity to present and compare the costs and benefits over the long-term of significant policies, as such comparisons are not done systematically. Compounding this, a predominant test on managerial competence is fiscal performance in balancing budgets over a short-term. Unless service quality is also monitored or the shifting of costs to consumers made transparent, then apparent efficiency gains from delivering more from managing within a financial budget are likely to be illusory.

There are few strong tests, and therefore insufficient thresholds of accountability for policy that would no longer meet basic value-for-money tests[4]. Recent rethinking of public sector discount rates reflects an overdue recognition that without some credible and relevant common metrics, the comparison of policy options will be unnecessarily pragmatic, particularly when assessing the comparative benefits of established programmes. Improved evaluation of new policies will not highlight the more significant policy risks and high opportunity costs to government of continuing existing policies long past their relevance.

The Public Finance Act 1989 provides the only formal obligation anywhere in government to consider the opportunity costs of deferred adjustment of policies to fit a changed context, although obligation is able to be delayed, should Ministers or Departments seek this. There is only anecdotal information about the deferred maintenance of public housing, schools, public hospitals and prisons in New Zealand, making any disclosure that finally occurs a question of integrity rather than transparency. In this vein, also of concern is the rewriting by government departments of their Briefings to Incoming Ministers once it was clear that the government would change after the general election of 2017 – this is contrary to the conventions about such briefings. Departments appear to have brought to the attention of the public since November 2017 an extra-ordinary range[5] of concerns that they had not previously acknowledged to the public.

The oversight of public administration by the Courts or the Ombudsman can be wide ranging. Where the performance of particular sectors is brought into question sufficiently often, or where maintaining confidence in them is of major political significance, special review bodies are sometimes put in place, for example the Independent Police Complaints Authority, the Health and Disability Commissioner and the Taxation Review Authority. These review bodies are able to make wide ranging recommendations on the performance of the entities they review and, in some cases, initiate court or other specified remedial action. Oversight bodies with a more substantive role are occasionally proposed for New Zealand, but generally they are not established. The Picot committee on Tomorrows Schools proposed an Education Commission which never got off the ground, and a similar outcome occurred when the Roper Review of Prisons in 2009 proposed a standing Sentencing Commission. There was for many years a Social Security Commission which was later abandoned. The Health sector has seen off such bodies as well. Some thirty years ago, there were strong financial arguments that because such independent bodies were at risk of departmental capture, they would simply become public advocates for more resources. This argument completely ignored the need to hold both Ministers and Departments to account in complex areas, where performance measures, fiscal oversight, management models and strategic plans were insufficient to oversee the complexity of connections, time-paths, forms of investment and volatility of the population base being served by these sectors of special importance to the lives of New Zealanders.

The other critical function in evaluation is that of the C&AG who is able to investigate whatever is needed to determine whether due process has been followed and whether entities have delivered their specified outputs (e.g. the 2009 review of the Ministry of Education: Managing support for students with high special educational needs[6]). But, it also needs to be recognised that this is a smaller part of the work of the C&AG whose core role is attesting to financial and non-financial reporting by public entities. The budget, and therefore the volume of this investigative work, is controlled by the Treasury.

The immediacy of response by the state sector to the different requirements of a new administration has usually occurred through the creation of new institutions[7]. The frequency of serial restructuring within existing departments and agencies across government is very high, and often follows the need for new programmes carried out by Ministerial departments. The expanding complexity in household structures, innovation in shared arrangements, diversity of business forms, the expanding range of services that can now be purchased, and the speed of product innovation, quickly render obsolete any rigid institutional arrangements when they are chosen to match government structures with the targets or area of policies.

Both Ministers and senior public servants have been slow to think beyond the existing model of public administration with its component autonomous agencies operating individually alongside an increasingly command and control form of Ministerial leadership. Several public sector initiatives including Better Public Services[8] have sought to bring about improvements without rethinking the basic model, despite the dominance in commercial entities operating in networked structures which place high value on information flows rather than a capacity to direct at a detailed level. Providing services that necessitate the integration of processes between agencies remains a fraught expectation, with approaches such as collective impact requiring sponsoring agencies to assume a degree of trust with contracted partners that severely tests the knowledge they have gained up to now about their sectors through narrow contracting models. The Chief Justice has recently challenged the constitutional integrity of proposals of the Ministry of Justice to limit the ways the Judges interact with offenders[9]. Untapped so far is the rich source of information within the Integrated Data Infrastructure (IDI)[10] about the connections made by citizens to government and funded agencies, and its possible influence on the role of agencies.

Difficulty in disentangling the actions of politicians from those of the public servant

The relationship between the political arm of the executive and the public service is specified in large part in statute, particularly the State Sector Act 1988. For specific functions (police, taxation, statistics etc.) this relationship may be defined more explicitly in legislation relating to that function. Vital for trust in public service is the impartial treatment of all citizens, and this is reinforced by recognition through the rule of law that the making of any law is separate from its administration. That constitutionally important boundary can be breached, or appear to be so, in several ways.

The public administration focus on accountability in serving the government of the day took a new turn in 1989 with the mantra 'the

Information and Institutions of Government Accountability

Minister is the client', which presumes that the Minister is the most relevant point for accountability to citizens for all transactions. This is embedded in the actions of public servants on the grounds that Ministers have been given a mandate to govern. The emergence of the 'no surprises' cabinet principle[11] and its acceptance without challenge conflates this fraught political/professional boundary. Because of this, when considering the performance of government, it is usually difficult to disentangle the actions of politicians from those of the public servants that ultimately give life to political choices and directions.

Conventionally, government has allocated activities to departments that are responsible for managing a service, community or relationship. The accountability of the public service has become redefined quite substantially in terms of its accountability to Ministers rather than citizens. This is less likely to occur where there is a statutory authority to act with some autonomy from ministerial direction, or where the processes of an organisation are subject to an independent review body. The merger of the National Archives into the Department of Internal Affairs, diminished the managerial heft of the Chief Archivist and his/her independent accountability to Parliament, is a good example of how statutory authority can nonetheless be changed when it suits the government.

The transparency of the relationship between public servants and Ministers requires expectations of and consequent potential challenge through the independent oversight by the House of Representatives, the Judiciary[12], the Ombudsman, independent bodies, Commissions of Inquiry, the media and civil society. Some countries have developed other means of making transparent the relationship between the public sector and Ministers, and New Zealand's adoption in 1981 of an Official Information Act followed similar obligations elsewhere. The 'no surprises' policy introduced into the cabinet manual may have diluted the impact of this earlier reform, as well as reducing Ministerial commitment to some long held conventions.

The arrangement of government that has developed since the Canterbury earthquakes of 2010 and 2011 showed with clarity the inseparability of politicians from public sector management processes. The Ministerial takeover of previously elected roles at Environment Canterbury. The recent surveillance legislation is another example of this. That such a close relationship should have developed may not be a surprise under the constitutional system in place, along with New Zealand's small population and the limits to other resources. Politicians have often preferred to place themselves as managers of the whole system of government, presenting the public service (bureaucrats[13]) and the Judiciary as obstacles to 'common sense' solutions that Ministers bring when they 'roll up their sleeves'.

Ministers have a tendency to seek to extend their involvement to managerial matters further broadening the pragmatic way in which key principles of the 1980's public sector reforms have been applied, particularly since the 1990s. As managers, Ministers have fewer levers to apply than have departmental heads, and they primarily involve budget setting, gate-keeping on cabinet proposals, board appointments, chief executive relationships and major changes to departmental structures. The amalgamation by Ministers of several supposedly underperforming departments into a larger government department, Ministry of Business, Innovation and Employment for instance, is a further example of the difficulty of maintaining consistency, as long as structural solutions are regarded as sufficient, although rarely optimal. Of consequence to public servants, but often unnoticed by the public, is the high cost of restructuring within agencies, where the initial costs in output loss and familiarisation by a new crop of second and third tier managers appointed by the chief executive of the time, is rarely recovered before the next restructure.

Executive government has extended for itself the conditions which enable Members of the Cabinet to 'get things done', often by limiting the available evidence base[14], and this can undermine longer term trustworthiness and effectiveness, as well as impartiality of the public service. This method of management by project underinvests in systems innovation and this is manifested in later shortcomings in capability and information to drive innovation. Policy choices are therefore limited. It also limits the scope of issues that need resolution to those aspects for which some understanding and means of a more immediate response exist.

Both the three-year term of Parliament and frustration with the inability of the public sector itself to grapple with politically challenging issues and bring about positive improvements to its contribution to society, lead Ministers to engage in managerial decisions. The counter argument to this statement is that initiatives can be put in place responsively, once there is a decision to take responsibility. This has become most likely where no one agency has a sufficiently comprehensive mandate for the identification and potential resolution of issues. In the social services sector there are many such emergent issues including: obesity; social media and technology; super diversity; suicide and self-harm; violence, abuse and bullying; mental health; drugs; pornography; antibiotic resistance; homelessness and crowding; fertility; urban infrastructure; incarceration costs; and third world diseases. The policy and programme oversight of family violence by leading Ministers in recent years is a significant and effective example where Ministerial leadership[15] had been critical in finally bringing about very necessary cross agency leadership and focus that was otherwise lacking.

The above comments remind us that policy will always have been chosen for political reasons, and that its operational oversight will often be shaped by those reasons. The necessity for the delivery of policy to citizens to be in an impartial manner requires developing an evidence base for operations that will be richer, more comprehensive and immediate than that used in policy development. The delivery of services to citizens in a trustworthy manner requires the service provider to have evidence to assure themselves *'of the standard to which those primary tasks and obligations are discharged, typically to third parties, and often to prescribed third parties*[16].

Where appropriate evidence has not been gathered to assess the performance of initiatives, more transparency is needed to explain why, and provide the public with knowledge about the limitations of the evidence and its consequences[17] for service quality.

The most serious consequence of not knowing the reliance that can be placed on evidence of any form used in public policy or service delivery is that it undermines the capacity of services to respond to change or of citizens to hold government to account. There is a higher likelihood that the wrong choices will be made. The resolution of such a dilemma requires the provision of appropriate information to communicate evidence of trustworthiness of the activities of the public sector effectively and usefully. The alternative is to underestimate the degree of uncertainty in what we know about ourselves, and the nature of change we are experiencing. Given the high trust that the New Zealand public has traditionally placed in government, the failure to signal uncertainties about the quality of services, whether they be directly provided or regulated, can mislead the public, business and regulators about the appropriate level of caution that they need to have.

Limited constitutional restraints on the executive

The public sector performance management system and its oversight by Select Committees and the C&AG place importance on the tests explicit and implicit in the Public Finance Act 1989 and State Sector Act 1988. After an initial decade of flexibility, innovation and occasional embarrassing incidents, the political and departmental management of risk has justified moves to expand ministerial monitoring, oversight and perhaps control of the processes that implement policy. The introduction into the Cabinet manual of the 'no surprises' principle encapsulated this unfortunate shift well. In the social services sector with so many transactions to oversee, this has resulted in Ministers and their departments: putting in place internal limits on departmental transaction risk; downplaying the external costs borne by citizens; forbidding of advocacy by funded community organisations; limiting autonomy at an operations level; and minimising forms of evaluation likely to reach the public domain. Consequently, when independent reviews such as the expert review of child protection services[18] take place, the findings inevitably reflect poorly on management practices that should have evolved much earlier with experience and feedback. 'No surprises' can also provide an opportunity for the staff of Ministers to indicate that the Minister might not wish to receive discoverable advice on some matters, about which she/he would be required to provide information if asked in the House of Representatives.

With little acknowledged recognition of the characteristics or needs of future generations of citizens and communities, much political achievement and institutional practice has been strongly focused on limiting the visibility of faulty process rather than lifting outcomes. There is now a legacy of limited in-depth policy evaluation and weak commitment to continuous improvement, particularly in the social services. Consequently, long-term deficiencies end up being obscured and can become difficult subsequently to respond to when they surface later, as has happened with institutional child abuse, leaky buildings, housing and water quality. Generally, regulations and other forms of authority have been designed to serve past representations of the communities to which they relate, yet the relevance of the investments that they influence will be needed to remain relevant in both the near and distant future. The capacity for continuous improvement and innovation is impaired by the lack of an evaluation culture, as is the capability to challenge and modify policy once in place, and the expectation of rapid response.

Government's capacity to change how it makes decisions is determined by the way that constitutional obligations affect the adaptability of vital institutions, including Parliament, Treasury, C&AG, and Governor-General. This is also the case with those other institutions that play a key part in trust in government. Changing how people get elected to Parliament through the adoption of MMP has not altered the fundamental nature of this enduring institution. The evolution of constitutional arrangements has brought new institutions, new roles and relationships. For enduring institutions, they have mainly facilitated a transformation of processes through information technology and reacted to periodic shifts in the fundamental 'world view' surrounding the operation and place of markets and social institutions. Despite this, the government of the day always has the ability to limit the scope of these arrangements through the budget appropriation process, by constrained funding[19]. For example, the number of value-for-money audits that the C&AG is able to undertake is determined by the appropriated funding, as are the inquiries of the Ombudsman.

In short, neither the capacity for thoughtful deliberation by executive government nor the scrutiny by the legislature has advanced in the face of the significant uncertainties the nation faces[20]. This is of concern when there are major uncertainties confronting the nation, the most apparent of which are from climate change, population change, land and water degradation, globalisation, introduction of harmful organisms, and new technologies, and the long-term incapacity to match New Zealand's wealth creation with that of other comparable nations.

Government effectiveness, as seen in the outcomes achieved when government decides to act, can range from the highly competent, to the inept. The introduction of the Goods and Services Tax (GST)[21], and the introduction of MMP point to a capacity to make highly significant system change in a short time, provided the policy is clearly thought through and responsibility clear. The immediate response to the Canterbury earthquake in February 2011 seemed at the time to have been extra-ordinarily effective, while the leaky homes (with an estimated cost of $11.3 billion to the nation)[22] reflect poorly on policy making, risk management and basic receptiveness to serious evidence justifying concern by citizens of the quality of regulatory and accreditation processes of central and local government.

Limited processes for deliberation – the case of intergenerational consequences

Governments will outlast even the most robust community and commercial entities. Within constitutional arrangements, motivations and constraints, the government of the day enacts laws, collects taxes, creates institutional structures, and applies these taxes. Laws, regulations, taxation, investment, disinvestment and social programmes can alter the comparative wellbeing of different generations. In the cases of health, education, welfare and retirement provision programmes this is an explicit intent.

The needs of future generations are rarely if ever those which generate issues for immediate action, although they are often compromised by the consequent policy response, which may be unfettered by any lack of knowledge of the issue. Intergenerational consequences of decisions are not always clear cut. Education has a benefit for the recipient and to society; it also has a benefit for future generations in a range of ways from increasing the wealth of the nation to being better parents. For some, better education also improves the likelihood that the recipient will emigrate taking the potential for these benefits with them. The intergenerational consequences often need scientific studies to understand, yet in the political domain the test is often of 'common sense', leading to policy by slogan. Given the political intensity of interest in the cross generational effects of conditions and policy in health, justice, education and welfare, the paucity of effective research in much of the social services makes these areas of policy more prone to swings of political fortunes than most other areas of policy.

The intergenerational ramifications of government decisions are primarily and often solely illustrated by fiscal comparisons. Public debt could simplistically be seen as the transfer of wealth from future generations to the present, whereas the assets owned by the Crown are a legacy from the investments of past taxpayers passed to present and future generations.

Where the economic position of households is such that child bearing is deferred, postponed or no longer intended, then a growing share of the reproductive capability will remain unused while production on the short term will lift. In the longer term, this will hasten the time in the demographic structure when deaths will exceed births. This transition has implications for the increasingly fragile regional population structures as well as ethnic diversity, housing and retirement provision, and the demographic profile of the labour market.

Citizens speak through the three-yearly election

A distinguishing feature of the New Zealand form of the Westminster model is that Parliament makes the rules and can change them to get things done. There are few, but well established, institutions to keep Government in check and these have specific constitutional roles. The ability to get things done quickly by the executive, as seen especially during the decade from 1984, has been followed by a return to a focus on near-term politics and policies.

The constitutional arrangements have been moulded over time to provide each new government with a high degree of ability to intervene in society, the economy and the environment. On the one hand this is done responsibly within the mandate of the party manifesto under which it was elected (modified by any coalition agreements with minor support parties), while on the other, in a way to maintain popularity. It has led to a high degree of oversight by government in society, economy and environment. This is particularly so in a pervasive public sector and high dependence of all sectors on the state, to the extent that the government is expected to intervene to underwrite the citizens' personal losses. Regulations put in place as a response to business failures, such as money laundering and potential firm closure[23], place huge demands on people and businesses which they are never likely to recoup[24].

The constitutional integrity of government stewardship is vital to the effective functioning of the public sector, as it should bring about transparency in how the interests of future generations are balanced, protect the integrity of judicial and electoral systems, and cause to be clear and visible the way that the state can contain the rights of its citizens through delineating the public interest. The guardians of the constitution include the Head of State, the legislature, executive and judicial limbs of government. The legislature consists of MPs who are supported in their role by the Officers of Parliament: C&AG, and several Parliamentary Commissioners and the Ombudsman. The executive branch includes elected parliamentarians, judicial-like appointments, commissions of inquiry, the State Services Commissioner and the appointed public service and numerous Crown entities. The judiciary comprises the permanent judiciary of the High Court and the mix of courts established by Parliament.

For elected parliamentarians, the broader capacity to challenge decision-making comes through Select Committees, Parliamentary questions and question time. Beyond the public sector, the C&AG, Royal Commissions of inquiry, autonomous public sector officials with statutory independence, permanent Commissioners such as those appointed for Environment, Health and Disability, Children, Human Rights and Race Relations have a distinct legislative basis for auditing and challenging decisions.

From the perspective of the franchised citizen, the form of the Westminster system of government operated in New Zealand has proven to be flexible to changes in the groups accommodated by constitutional arrangements and how these groups participate in government. It has proved to be less responsive in: the adaptivity of the institutions of government; the processes for deliberation; and the effectiveness of government. These features of the New Zealand form of the Westminster system pose significant challenges for holding government to account. For example, identifying the groups being accommodated and those being excluded; making transparent the impact of the accommodation e.g. through veto power or allocation of resources; and in the trustworthiness of government institution e.g. are some groups getting unfair benefit or bearing undue cost from government actions. Against this background, ultimately citizens speak for themselves and their community of interest through the three-yearly election.

A summary of the purposes of existing roles that hold government to account

The capacity to hold the government of the day to account on behalf of citizens depends on how the place of the role or attribute is embedded in the constitution as it is, in statutes and conventions around particular long-established roles and processes, and in an evolving mix of mechanisms established to provide redress of some sort. It also includes the operational practices of organisations intended for evaluation and continuous improvement, the way systems of organisations are connected and evolve, and the accumulation of knowledge and its accessibility.

The range of mechanisms that have developed in New Zealand are:

1. Oversight of constitutional system:

- The Governor-General as Head of State
- Parliament
- Judiciary
- Controller and Auditor-General
- State Services Commissioner
- Solicitor-General

- Defence Force
- Treaty of Waitangi

2. Underpinning the rule of Law:

- Commissioner of Police
- Commissioner of Inland Revenue
- Chief Electoral Officer
- Registrar of Births Deaths and Marriages
- Land Information Registrar
- Inspector-General of Intelligence and Security
- Ombudsman

3. Ensuring trustworthiness of information:

- Government Statistician
- Royal Society
- Chief Scientist
- Controller and Auditor-General

4. Protecting rights:

- Waitangi Tribunal
- Children's Commissioner
- Human Rights Commissioners
- Environment Commissioner
- Director-General of Health
- International conventions

5. Trusted special studies of irregular outcomes such as deaths:

- Coroners
- Royal Commissions

6. System for regulation, complaints and redress:

- Ombudsman
- Health and Disability Commissioner
- Independent Police Complaints Authority
- Financial Markets Authority
- Ministry for Consumer Affairs
- Worksafe New Zealand
- Commerce Commission

7. Public administration:

- Departments of State including Treasury
- Free and frank advice conventions
- Fiscal responsibility statutory obligations
- Parliamentary commissions
- Select Committees
- Parliamentary questions
- Productivity Commission

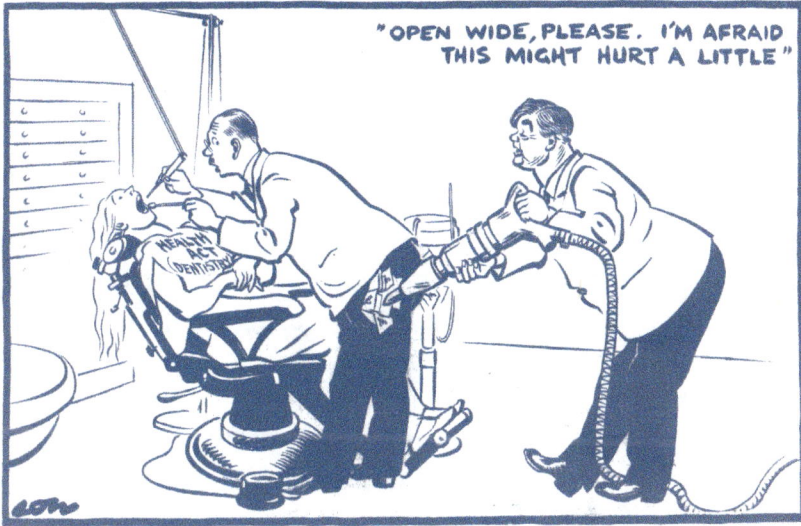

"OPEN WIDE, PLEASE. I'M AFRAID THIS MIGHT HURT A LITTLE"

Chapter 2
Mechanisms to hold government to account

The trustworthiness of government

There are two elements to accountability[25]: first, to improve trustworthiness through intelligently designed systems of accountability which check and provide evidence of claims and commitments; and second, to help individuals place and refuse trust intelligently by providing intelligible and usable information on trustworthiness. To hold government to account in this way, we have adopted the concept 'come-at-ability'[26], which explains how easy it is for the citizen to 'come-at' government. This form of accountability is founded on the obligation of government to be trustworthy, and for citizens to be able to come-at government for its decisions and behaviour. It does not rest on organisational structures and governance arrangements. Nor does it need communities to require a 'seat at the table' to gain decision-making power to hold government to account. Accountability rests on the provision of information to check and provide evidence of claims and commitments of government.

It is important for governments to maintain the trust of citizens because failure of trust in government impoverishes society, economy and environment as a whole – even though there may be a few winners. This burden imposed by government is the deadweight loss to the nation. There is a myriad of ways that deadweight loss is increased by government actions. It is increased by: the inability to anticipate the foreseeable by underinvestment in information; constraints on evaluation, limited investment in continuous improvement initiatives; and inadequately informed political oversight of managerial functions[27]. It is also increased by a system of executive government which limits the capacity of society, economy and environment, for example, by the loss of rich knowledge that develops insight; imposing high transaction costs, by making long-term investment in discovery and innovation unattractive; and imposing personal losses on people by tolerating poor policy outcomes. An illustration of the large impact of this deadweight loss on society, economy and environment was the reduced capacity for early detection of system failures which was then manifested in the costs of rectifying leaky buildings.

Deadweight losses are also increased by inefficient and ineffective public sector management, for example, in terms of poor value network leadership, and through failure to explicitly manage foreseeable risks[28]; and under-investment in infrastructure[29]. In addition, deadweight losses are increased by the institution of government services that are inappropriate to the intended task and drive perverse behaviours[30] or crowd alternatives out of the market. The institution of government services that provide no meaningful capability for users to intelligently place or refuse trust in these services, especially where they impose punitive measures on users who attempt to withdraw from the use of these services, also increases deadweight loss.

Fusing political representation with impartial and effective services for all citizens

It is fundamental to democracy that politicians can be elected from ordinary citizens, without a need to demonstrate eligibility by meeting prior tests of skill, aptitude, judgement or even community standards of integrity. The level of trust in the politicians that have formed the government of the day will wax and wane during their tenure. Public confidence in the systems of government, and the capacity to maintain functions fundamental to ensuring the integrity of the state both need to be sustained regardless of trust in the persons who form the elected executive of the day and determine policy. The State cannot function well were its citizens to withdraw trust in the operation of the police, the tax system, the justice system, and many other functions of government because of the qualities of the Minister in charge. To guard against that possibility, government needs to be organised to demonstrate trustworthiness by whatever means available that are sufficiently far-reaching and robust so as to justify and ensure confidence in the integrity, fairness and impartiality of services and the upholding of the law. Critical to this is transparency in the relationship between Ministers and the Public Service.

Embedded in the Public Service Act 1912 were the key foundations for trustworthiness in the management and operation of government's business: the appointment of public servants on merit, independent of politicians, who have no personal commercial or financial gain from public transactions. Public service legislation since 1912 has had the intention of separating the operation of the institutions of government from the politics of governing the country, but not always the assessment of their performance. One of the implications of a public service employed on merit is that it can recognise the importance of meeting international standards and conventions, enforce managerial and scientific excellence, provide assurance of commercial integrity of markets (labour, finance, land, commodities etc.), and remain trusted by the opposition as much as the government[31].

The State Sector Act 1988 destroyed the concept of a unified public service, although the amendments in 2013 partially reintroduced this. With these statutes, it is decisions of the prime minister of the day that shape how the machinery of government operates in practice, as they try to integrate the needs of politics, policy and administration into sufficient alignment to allow effective government. Each government has its own way of enhancing the relative influence of ministers with officials[32].

Irrespective of such machinery of government considerations, the small size of New Zealand, the dominance of central government in national affairs, and a history of high trust in government has resulted in government being the prime and often sole source of information by which the public can hold government to account. Questions of the accountability of the government for its decisions regularly appear in the media. News headlines are typically in the context of the lack of transparency of government actions in regard to the funding of schools, medicines and hospital care; the inability to tackle domestic violence; or making incorrect/'inappropriate' payment to beneficiaries.

Government dedicates considerable resources to the production of the evidence that it chooses, so as to demonstrate its performance. Examination of these performance measures shows them to often narrow attention to particular results that have gained prominence to enable the government of the day to define how it seeks to have its achievements portrayed. The privileging of some forms of evidence often results in more relevant forms of evidence either not being produced or made available. While there are many in the state involved in overseeing the flow of information, most noticeable of these are the resources dedicated to communications roles[33]. Ministers and departments can withhold evidence, by delaying finalisation or publication, deferring release indefinitely or withholding authority for evidence to be prepared.

There are some special roles as arbiters of government information, most notably the Judiciary, C&AG, and Government Statistician, as well as the Chief Science Advisor and the Royal Society. These accountability mechanisms are important to a small democracy with limited resources where poor government decisions are costly and deeply impact the capacity and resilience of society, the economy and the environment. There are others with independence in preparing and releasing information akin to the Government Statistician, including the Parliamentary Commissioner for the Environment. Apart from the organisations that are guided by statute in how information is prepared and released, the absence of strong, transparent public sector-wide conventions about the preparation and release of scientific research studies means that the independent timing and form of release of such material has become dependent on the personal relationship between individual agency heads and their Minister. Consequently, agencies cannot commit in advance to the availability of research findings, however influential or important they will be. The Treasury is the most notable exception to this observation whereas the performance of other major agencies is patchy.

The systematised accumulation of appropriate information builds the knowledge essential to anticipate or to react so as to make progress in the face of change in social, economic and environmental conditions. Holding government to account for how it is itself managed as a knowledge centre, strengthens trust in government as well as strengthening its constitutional integrity. It is an especially important role in New Zealand where such a large share of the information needed to hold government to account is in its hands.

Holding government to account as a knowledge centre covers well known information on the condition of society, economy and environment, as well as information on policies. Such information pinpoints the questions that we need to address about ourselves as a society. It also covers information to assess government's performance and information produced to enable stakeholders to place or refuse trust in public services. Such information points to the options we might have to change the condition we are in. From the perspective of citizens, government performance also reflects compliance costs, transaction costs, penalties for non-compliance, risk bearing, the nature of the deadweight loss from rigid public sector institutions, and the management of intergenerational exchanges. Such accountability involves the existence of evidence as well as the establishment of the appropriate means of producing evidence given the nature of the service and its impact on citizens.

Retrospective mechanisms include those where citizens can provide feedback, which include continuous learning practices, as well as forensic processes of coroners, judicial reviews and special inquiries. Natural experiments are unintended outcomes or conditions which bring information that would never otherwise be gleaned. Examples in New Zealand include disasters such as the Canterbury earthquakes of 2011. Regrettably, many of these mechanisms are not applied comprehensively, or are applied ineffectually[34]. The consequence of this is that the full potential of evidence-based policy formulation processes that are dependent on the thoughtful accumulation of information, however simple, has not been realised.

In practice, sometimes government makes decisions with limited information because of political imperatives to act, or to be seen to act. These can easily become situations where, perversely, governments have used their authority to limit the availability or delay access to appropriate information. This can inhibit the capacity of citizens to come-at government or enable a later more effective response[35]. Where Ministers become part of the final stages of release of statistical or research studies, as is occasionally their wont, it risks generating uncertainty in the public about the possibility of engagement in the content itself, hence ministerial involvement can reduce trust not only in the information but generally in all involved with it.

Reduced trustworthiness can also be associated with the unmanaged fragmentation of public service processes, along with self-referencing performance assessment, rigid contracting practices, a narrowed codification of people, and a history of poor investment in analytical and evaluation capability. Where these issues occur, it demonstrates poor systems level thinking capability within the public sector. A consequence of this is poor utilisation of the potential information resources available to government. When the drivers of change are many[36], the response of government to those things that could influence the nature, scope and form of government will depend on how well and at what cost it can adapt. Where government is seen to have become less effective or not earned the trust of citizens, then the levers familiar to politicians may lose effectiveness.

A strength of New Zealand's constitutional arrangements is that once elected a government has few impediments to fulfilling its manifesto commitments, subject only to how it manages to maintain its majority in the Parliament and the rule of law. The weakness of the constitutional arrangements is that the obligations for effective deliberation before implementation of policies are quite inadequate, with the consequence that there are limited mechanisms for ensuring the robustness and longevity of policy once the executive changes.

This concern is seen in other Westminster systems of government, including Australia and the United Kingdom. In all these places, the visibility of concerns has increased about the reduced willingness of politicians to receive free and frank advice from their officials in ways that are transparent. Other institutions cannot be relied on to fill this deficiency in information. New Zealand has few opportunities from

Parliamentary challenge or select committees, the media, an upper house or independent research houses which could provide some compensation for this. That this is not impossible to achieve is exemplified by the Waitangi Tribunal, which has stimulated a wealth of historical research into the interactions between Māori and the emerging New Zealand state, and provided a trustworthy basis for long awaited partial redress for misdeeds of the past.

The framework covering information provided by government

For decision-making a wide spectrum of sources of information are used:

- Scientific studies whose purpose is to uncover new knowledge.
- Quantitative data from operational sources (e.g. number and type of intendents and transaction, number of people involved and for how long, people's sentiment and service quality experience, costs etc.) and collections of industry, capital markets and national statistics. In most cases this information is useful to provide the context to which they apply, but, is usually unsuitable for identifying emerging trends.
- Case study and qualitative research. This frequently takes the form of market research and is most useful in elaborating current players in the market and opinions towards those players, and alternatives available. A particular problem with this form of information is that the results tend to be biased, frequently introduced in the selection of respondents.
- Mathematical models that summarise data and enable trends to be extrapolated.
- Operational information, exemplified by that from user feedback and continuous improvement processes.
- Client feedback, from complaints, focus groups, consumer surveys.
- Accumulated experience of experts in a specific domain. This is frequently called on where no or limited data is available or where the data are ambiguous and needs interpretation.

- Ad hoc independent external inquiry into particular services, such as the Expert Review of Child Protection, the reviews of the Productivity Commission, and occasional Royal Commissions or Boards of Inquiry.
- Independent reviews by the Ombudsman.
- Anecdote and hearsay. Sometimes relied on heavily, particularly when presented in the form of scenario analysis.
- The spirit of the time, or zeitgeist, in which there is wide-spread views about, for example, trends in society, economy and environment. Most recently this has been seen with the range of reasons given for the housing bubble, which have ranged from the impact of foreign speculators, to unsuitable urban planning constraints.

Information about government performance comes in the form of official statistical information, publicly funded research, academic studies, international studies, community-based research, international benchmarking, other research and intelligence, alongside well-planned enquiries, and reflection and analysis that need long lead times and are derived from knowledge and insights. Official statistics create the means to identify: the questions that need to be asked about the most concerning social, economic and environmental issues facing New Zealand; their nature; and ways to address them. In this sense, Official Statistics are a precondition to the systematic development of evidence for identifying issues of concern, improving understanding of those issues, contributing to the development of solutions, and informing decision-making.

Information influences confidence about the future, and the directions set. How this information is accumulated, and how much is available is reflected in judgments, insights, and models. The extent of information available impacts the ability to cope with future policy questions and concerns, the opportunity costs, risks and range of alternatives, as well as expectation about the continued significance of current issues.

This view of information can be described as 'scientific' in that there is a structured approach to gathering and applying evidence behind it and a method for assessing risk and drawing inferences. Scrutiny of scientific work is provided by robust peer review processes. Statistics offices are subjected to these review processes and in addition, to provide safeguards, most governments confer statutory independence on the statistical office in the methods to be used, and the impartiality of the release of results.

This view carries the notion that information on performance and the analysis of performance is both useful and valuable. It can be used to examine the efficiency, effectiveness and efficacy of public sector services, such as their use of resources to deliver outputs, the quality and reach of the outputs they deliver, their effectiveness and impact on society, economy and environment.

Scientific information is also used for policy analysis and evaluation for example through reviewer centric methods, systems-based methods and researcher-based methods. Scientific information is frequently incomplete and sometimes ambiguous, and without associated measures of uncertainty this can limit trust in its usefulness. Prospective mechanisms to use this information usually involve some analytically based modelling capability founded on the structured accumulation of information. The size of the economic base and weak inherent commitment to research determines the extent of availability of information for this which may explain the observed weak capacity for this in New Zealand.

There are noticeable instances where planning bodies with supporting research capacity have been put in place by government but later abandoned, for example the Monetary and Economic Council (1961-1978), Planning Council (1979-1991), National Development Council (1969-1974), and Public Health Commission (1993-1995). The

Productivity Commission established in 2011 follows the success in Australia of a similar body. This situation compares starkly with the situation in the United Kingdom where robust challenge takes place through a large mix of independent research centres, many with a long history of challenging public policy. The absence of an ongoing community of independent research centres, or some substitute that fits New Zealand's resource base, leaves a weakened capacity or desire to reason and contribute to public policy formulation. With a weaker capacity or desire to reason the government has become poorly placed to address the nature of the issues faced by governments.

Along with the Productivity Commission, the most politically robust mechanism for this within the public sector is provided by Treasury's four yearly Statement on New Zealand's Long-term Fiscal Position. Despite the willingness to highlight tensions in the long-run sustainability of current policy, this regular statement needs to be seen in comparison with the United Kingdom situation where long-term strategic statements are more likely to be underpinned by extensive and rigorous major independent reviews by leading experts. Reports from these reviews form reference resources for subsequent analysis. This also applies to the work of the National Audit Office whose well researched value-for-money studies add to the overall understanding of the impact of public policy decisions in the United Kingdom.

The reports by leading experts in New Zealand in comparison are uneven in the quality of their analysis, which can be a reflection of the simplistic view Ministers can have about the time needed for a robust inquiry[37]. Where insightful studies have been completed, follow up is often poor and inadequate response given to the substance of the findings[38]. Despite these potential shortcomings, examples such as the Family Violence Death Review Committee reports from the Health and Safety Commission and some external research consultants[39] are examples that have had a profound effect on policy analysis.

Where there are insufficient mechanisms for engaging with thinkers outside the public sector, the less likelihood there is that the current or future context of policy will be well understood, or that assumptions and judgements inherent in policy making will be subject to adequate scrutiny and validation.

There is strong pressure from the media and the opposition for Governments to provide instant answers to newsworthy issues, with little quarter given when uncertainty or imperfection is acknowledged. The pressure imposed by the 24-hour news cycle, supposedly needed to feed an unforgiving electorate, may fundamentally change the political accountability processes. There are instances when this appears to have resulted in poor quality policy responses, and poor decisions when commitments are unchanged.

How the electorate assesses the claims and commitments of government is also influenced by press releases from Ministers and public sector press offices which seek to portray any situation as most favourable to the government. There are some safeguards on this provided by key legislation that places information reporting requirements on the various officers of Parliament, particularly the Electoral Act 1993, Official Information Act 1982, Public Finance Act 1989, Public Audit Act 2001, and Statistics Act 1975. In the application of legislation, there is ample evidence[40] that much of the information actually provided is interpreted to suit the government of the day. As has already been noted, the weaknesses in government accountability mechanisms, such as the absence of an upper house, are not balanced by other processes. A more cynical view is that "so what, government does not have the resources to do anything too radical in a three-year term of Parliament".

Institutional rigidities in the use of information

Information for open, informed, objective challenge to recognised wisdom of the nature of government, society and commerce, and the pressures and opportunities that they currently and potentially face is limited within executive government. For example, Select Committees have sometimes been chaired by a Minister. This situation compares starkly with the situation in the United Kingdom where robust challenge takes place through well-resourced mechanisms, such as the Commons Select Committees. There, it is not unusual for government backbenchers to behave independently of their party position when assessing legislation. Where Select Committees seek information to challenge policy and operational choices, then how the accountability of departmental officials to Parliament is distinct from their responsibility to Ministers remains somewhat blurred, although anticipation of possible tension may influence how advice to Ministers is framed.

As a contrast to practices in New Zealand, in the United Kingdom the independence of the speaker of Parliament is long established, independent analysis groups exist, such as the Kings Fund, Rowntree Foundation, the Institute of Economic Affairs, the Institute for Fiscal Studies, and the Royal Institute of International Affairs. The House of Lords Committees provide further challenge. To reinforce this contrast, as Speaker from 2008 to 2013, the Hon. Lockwood-Smith had required Ministers of the Crown to provide informative answers to an extent not seen in the Parliament for some decades – this is a low bar for accountability.

How Ministers meet as a Cabinet is critical to their accountability. Where major decisions in any portfolio are made by Cabinet, then Ministers need to have the backing of their peers, and implicitly ministerial choices will be informed by the best advice from several relevant departmental experts, rather than officials of the sponsoring department. The opportunity for cross agency study on the impact for government as whole, and communities beyond those normally reached by the sponsoring department can be highly beneficial. For the public sector, cabinet solidarity reduces the potential for departments with common agenda and obligations to receive conflicting directions from departmental Ministers, which potentially narrows the range of available solutions. Little is known about the influence of different cabinet decision-making styles on holding to account Ministers and departments.

Institutional rigidity is caused by the retrospective nature of most of the monitoring mechanisms. A consequent focus on static efficiency by backward-looking inspection comes at the expense of both dynamic and allocative efficiency. Static efficiency refers to a focus on short-term concerns with no or very limited consideration of long-term consequences. Dynamic efficiency relates to the ability to quickly and at low cost adapt to maintain outputs and productivity to changes in conditions, such as globalisation. The benefit from changing the apportionment or distribution of resources is assessed by the concept of allocative efficiency. Market failure is frequently a cause of allocative inefficiency. The advancement of social investment by a former Minister of Finance[41] was a clear signal of political dissatisfaction with the existing mechanisms for the provision of social services, and this concern has been reinforced by the findings of the Productivity Commission[42] on social services and the Expert Review of Child Protection[43].

Assessing efficacy and effectiveness requires evaluative practices that can be costly, and these appear to have required Ministerial endorsement, which seems to be given rarely. In some quarters this has been regarded as heightening political and departmental risks, thereby reducing the propensity to undertake such assessments[44]. Furthermore, the nature of technological transformation focused on real-time information management with the potential for sophisticated information modelling, scanning and linking has concentrated activity in highly integrated key institutional, national and global infrastructures. The business transformation, core competencies and relationship management necessitated by these shifts, and the associated real-time consumer interactions are most unlikely to be adopted in organisations that lack effective consumer links or a quality management culture. This is reflected in the limited commitment to collective impact projects, as seen in the poor support for Whanau Ora by the major Ministries.

The development of politically appointed intermediaries who sift the information from departments on behalf of Ministers brings rigidities to the relationship between ministers and senior staff of government agencies. There is a vital place for interaction between Ministers and senior public servants. Ministers gain free and frank advice about the operations of the departments they are responsible for. From these exchanges, senior public servants gain insights about the thinking behind cabinet choices. Strategic insights are more often gained by experienced public servants from such interactions than through formal internal planning processes.

Instead, where Ministers place their own advisors on their office staff as intermediaries it can complicate the ability of senior public servants giving free and frank advice derived from the resources available to their departments, particularly when the standing of advisors is very high with ministers for reasons other than analytical competence. Indeed, under this arrangement public servants can be judged by their ability to provide advice that was supported by minister's advisors and acceptable to ministers. This may have led to a shift in how far there is prior referral to Ministers to decide on the advice they wish to receive formally from officials. Limiting the interaction between Ministers and public servants has uncertain consequences for the quality of advice. The balance between written and oral advice continues to shift, with suggestions that written advice is more likely to be given in a form which endorses the prior views of Ministers[45].

In providing advice to ministers, the Department of Prime Minister and Cabinet, Treasury and State Services Commission have the role of pooling the advice of officials to articulate a whole of government service view. In formulating their advice, the Department of Prime Minister and

Cabinet also advises on the likely response by key stakeholders, including parties outside of the public sector such as lobby groups and citizens.

The unique constitutional position of Māori creates an obligation to monitor the position of Māori and to respond to what is found. The Māori population has different demographic characteristics, is spread differently around New Zealand and has different family and community structures through whānau and hapū. Māori experience outcomes in health, education and employment that are outside the norm of those systems that deliver services to the whole of the nation. Past history has been to apply solutions that placed little importance on long-term remedies relevant to the position of Māori or their place in their determination and application. As recognition of the constitutional obligations of the state to these communities has risen, so too have the expectations that the distinct character of Māori would be more broadly recognised not only in policy but in its evaluation and monitoring. The Treaty places obligations on the Crown, and the Crown is usually the agent of the various means by which the Crown is held to account. Official statistics are one of these means, so there needs to be some mechanism of holding government of the day to account for what is the scope and form of official statistics, and how matters integral to Māori as a Treaty partner are treated in these statistics.

In a similar vein, the Pacific communities of New Zealand bring a wide range of cultures to New Zealand. The development of rules and practices for their communities often presumes a similarity (reinforced in much past social research and public policy) that defies their history. Similarly, the term Asian obscures the huge differences between Indian, Chinese, Malaysian, Thai, Japanese and Korean cultures, and among them as well. The past apparent homogeneity of most of New Zealand can no longer be depended on as a basis for uninformed and untested presumption of need, acceptance or trust by citizens.

In as far as politicians are concerned about informed debate, they too are interested in scientific information. When formulating public policy, politicians' interests are framed by their perspective on matters that influence the role of the state (e.g. universality versus targeting, and rehabilitative versus punitive).

Politicians are also concerned about information on public interest, political coalitions, and what works. Political decisions are made, and political actions taken, for the purposes of achieving political objectives. In making such decisions, Ministers are aware to a greater extent than public officials (depending on the information available and the acuity of the Ministers) of what kinds of choices are likely to seem acceptable. Myths and stories that are often not supported by evidence are used by politicians as a way to gain political support. There are no sanctions for inaccurate representations of complex social, economic and environmental situations by politicians in the cut and thrust of politics.

Where a decision impacts significantly on the interests of a vocal lobby group, Ministers will be very aware of the likely response of that group when making the decision. Where the decision affects the general public widely, Ministers will be aware of the likely reaction of the public and the likely response of opposition politicians, the media, and informed commentators. Where a decision requires political support, Ministers will be cognisant of the expectations of those whose support they will need. Politics is a mixed game played under uncertainty – in part against nature, in part against other players, and in part together with other players. And information will be called on for this purpose. Information will also be used as evidence by opposing players to attack and undermine this position.

A corollary of this is that without evidence to elucidate the position of a community of interest, its interests are less likely to be explicitly taken into account. The propensity to enable policy by slogan can often constrain the options available to politicians, particularly where some purportedly moral foundation exists for an otherwise ill-informed position. This is especially important in Justice policy where punitive responses tend to strike an accord with the public more than rehabilitative options. The ease with which a minor party backbencher was able to have sufficient support for the 'Three strikes and you're out' legislation was followed by later legislation that was supported by all the major political parties to tighten bail laws. This was despite the immediate negative impact on the already catastrophic incarceration rates of young Māori men. The regulatory impact statement by the Ministry of Justice for this law change grossly underestimated the additional numbers of prisoners that would result, or the more significant consequences for Māori[46].

The role of judicial processes to hold government to account

Judicial processes play an important role because Government, as with other entities, must operate within the law. The courts are adept at dealing with conclusions drawn from analyses utilising assemblages of disparate sources of information. In some cases, judicial processes have documented information which have wider uses, for example, breaches to the Treaty of Waitangi Tribunal pursued through the Māori Land Court. As Dame Sean Elias has observed:

> *Sometimes the obligation to say what the law is brings the judiciary into collision with the executive. It is often overlooked that a principal virtue of the supervisory jurisdiction of the courts over executive action is to provide authoritative vindication for what has been done, stilling controversy. While from time to time some heat may be generated in decisions of the courts which displease the executive, this function is the constitutional responsibility of the courts under the rule of law[47].*

While judicial processes can be an effective method of holding government to account on specific breaches of law, they can be

Information and Institutions of Government Accountability

costly to use. This cost on the one hand provides a barrier to challenging government, as well as an unequal setting when the government agencies have access to the resources of the state to sustain their position in a court of law. This is especially critical with sanctions and penalties that apply solely to benefit recipients or prisoners, where any abuse of process is unlikely to be able to be challenged because of disproportionate procedural costs.

Governments authority to deliver on commitments not matched with a framework of information

New Zealand's constitutional arrangements have given the executive government considerable authority with few constraints if it wishes to act with an immediacy that appears impossible in countries with more complex systems. The responsiveness of government is coming under an increasing degree of real-time scrutiny, because others have an ever-expanding capacity to juxtapose opinions, advice and judgments from different places, interest groups and periods, without the necessity for balance of any form. This problem extends to organisations concerned with market integrity such as the Reserve Bank. Politicians have had to become used to engaging in this context, responding regardless of their preparation, even though quite often their responses can lead to long-term commitments[48]. This has always been in the nature of politics, but it has been amplified dramatically by contemporary media, the internet and contemporary communications systems.

Recent technologies now bring a real-time inter-activeness of almost all media, but there are generational differences in expectations of their use and authority. Few in the public service have stepped up to this form of scrutiny. In this respect, the political and professional arms of the executive do not share equally at the front line in bringing accountability for what government does. The responsiveness of the public service is more often to support the responsiveness of politicians, rather than to ensure the appropriate accountability of all arms of the executive, and this balance of responsibility will differ with the source of concern.

Determining what can be trusted is critical to democracy when so much is produced by government, in the face of temptations by the executive of the day to use the processes that they oversee to political advantage. Central to holding government to account is evidence of: condition of society, economy and environment; effectiveness of policies; government performance; and the capacity of citizens to intelligently place and refuse trust. There are mechanisms at the constitutional level for citizens to be able to come-at government.

When governments change, they have the authority to deliver on their commitments with few constraints. This flexibility is not matched by consequent accountability as there are limitations on the ability of individuals to intelligently place and refuse trust in government, mainly due to the opacity surrounding many of its operational elements.

THE LITTLE THING THAT PUZZLES HIM.

Chapter 3

Impact of changes in velocity of circulation of information and network processes

Sources of information on government policy

Information sources that play a part in political life include: celebrity opinion, fiction and unusual personal experience; newspaper coupon surveys and internet surveys; opinion polls; political events in other countries; monitoring of special groups, religious opinion and ideological positions; community statistics; Government Statistics; and academic research studies and peer reviewed international scientific findings.

An increasing range of competing information, of varying significance, reliability, velocity of circulation, accessibility and communicability is becoming more available. Much of this is from the large collections of administrative data which governments generate in the course of their operational activities. As access is evolving with technological innovation and new approaches to media management, the mix of information sources that dominates public attention, and hence political life, is changing the nature, speed and deliberation of decision-making. The potential origin of easily accessed information sources can be global, national or local. Increasing emphasis is being place on 'easy to get at' evidence.

The demands on policy making are also increasing. These demands are changing the mix of information sources that dominate public attention, and hence political life, as well as the nature, speed and deliberation of decision-making.

Much new information comes by way of data that has been codified in some way to enable rapid integration with data from other sources. Managing the meta data and developing rules around codified information for application by staff with limited autonomy requires recognition of the limits to the simplifying nature of models in the face of the complexity of people as subjects to classify. The capacity for statistical models to increase predictive capability about particular interventions needs the counterweight of informed operational autonomy, or other forms of validation.

Models and algorithms are increasingly used for screening, and to date, they have been left to operational managers to oversee the integrity in their own areas. Despite their potential impact on citizens, there are no government-wide standards for assessing the integrity of automated screening processes. Such standards should cover the validity of computational practices given classification and measurement error, sample representativeness and randomness, contextual relevance of data used, population variability, theoretical foundations and statistical integrity.

Society's adoption of developments resulting from highly accessible information and communications technology has given rise to new sources of data that are amenable to statistical methods and able to create useful information of high value – access to which people and organisations are prepared to pay. These administrative sources generated by operational processes, have been shown to have very strong benefits from network processes, especially in the private sector. If government were to invest in knowledge systems to exploit the current and emerging opportunities in information and communications technology, then the velocity of information could be increased, and information made more widely available. The effective use of this information requires a richer inferential capability, matching quantitative and computational skills with statistical competence, both of which depend on a strong commitment to measuring uncertainty. Uncertainty is an essential knowledge resource, influencing the shape of services, structures and engagement practices of service delivery.

Velocity of circulation of information

The velocity is the rate with which that information dominates the attention of the media and commentators, and hence political life. Velocity increases with attributes such as: the breadth of potential places and sources for such information; making the information 'real' by associating it with situations of identifiable people; the apparent relevance of generalising from specific cases to the population at large; the recentness of the information i.e. breaking news; and the uniqueness of the story in terms of its human interest or political agenda.

Despite the richer analytical possibilities that information and communications technologies bring, the place of scientifically founded evidence in the media and hence political life is steadily diminished by the rapidly expanding array of alternative information, much based on the global circulation of local anecdotes of high human interest. Whereas the information generated by scientific studies may add to our understanding of the subject, it may do little to generate a human-interest story or advance a political agenda. One exception comes from the meteorological field, where emergent technologies to source, analyse and present scientific information have made high velocity information understandable and available to the general public in the form of weather forecasts. This capacity to integrate auxiliary information into models can bring a real-time responsiveness to an expansive array of related information regardless of its form or frequency, with applications ranging from the local to global. Perversely, in an attempt to give scientific studies a human-interest twist, the results can be oversimplified and presented as deterministic relationships, for example, the news headline: 'Researchers can predict 3-year olds' future problems' reporting on the Dunedin Longitudinal Study[49].

A key strength of sound policy analysis is the influence on policy decisions of the understanding of variability and representativeness in the information on which policy is based. This challenges any reliance on determinism in the selected dataset. Societies, such as in New Zealand, are made up of an increasing diverse range of communities and individuals as a consequence of: migration; social change including the loss of old norms; globalisation on where people can work, trade and live; urbanization; fertility and family differences; and increasing longevity.

Fastly increasing velocity of information poses a challenge to the capacity to assess its quality. This is a serious concern, as sources that have the highest velocity are generally of unknown and limited quality. The increase in number of high velocity sources could have the effect of crowding out relevant scientific work where analytical resources are limited as well as affecting its visibility. Compounding this, it can be difficult to explain simply the comparative uncertainty associated with different results. That share of policy development contributing to public policy that is justified by information sources that have a high risk of being challenged will rise with the velocity of information.

Whilst public policy most often involves the balancing of short-term costs and long-term benefits, there is a risk that the higher the velocity of information, the greater the visibility and hence political intensity of interest in short-term costs. The disproportionate emphasis on these means that political explanations of the balance between costs and benefits can be somewhat volatile. Long-term policies tend to poorly reflect the interests of populations whose visibility is better reflected more in scientific studies. Policy change when made has a high likelihood of being temporary. Vacillation by political parties, across the spectrum, over the age of eligibility for new superannuation, offending policy or the resolution of low value housing shortages, typifies the dilemma politicians face in such situations.

Many political preferences are formed not with strong evidence but by reactions to the public's interest of the moment, as well as in the heat of elections or coalition formation. Thus, as well as being disproportionately underused in policy development, scientific study is inadequately valued.

The institutions that have the potential to provide a counterbalance for this may be harder to maintain in a nation with a smaller population. There is a small but not independent research and analytical capability in the public sector. Commercial goals of Crown Research Institutes and their competitive nature as with universities (with the exception of the Centres of Research Excellence) through Performance Based Research Funds focus on researcher excellence bring little capacity to link research to long-term questions of performance. Where outcomes have been specified, they risk being based on politically visible aspirations rather than the most relevant issues for New Zealand. The inception of Social Policy Research and Evaluation Unit as a Crown Agency focused on evaluation in 2013 was followed in 2017 by its planned abandonment. Such a pathway had been followed earlier by the closure of the Social Science Bureau of the DSIR in 1938, disestablishment of the Social Research Crown Research Institute in 1995, and the ending of the Planning Council in 1991, amongst others[50].

As well as being disproportionately underused in policy development, scientific study is inadequately valued. Scientific institutions have been slow to recover lost ground in this competition for media and citizen attention. The institutions that have the potential to provide a counterbalance for this may be harder to maintain for nations with small populations.

The role of the scientist in public life has become increasingly important for informed debate and public understanding, yet there is a decline in the number of public sector leaders of standing among the scientific community who can do this[51]. The appointment of a Chief Science Advisor to the Prime Minister in 2009, and the later development of departmental science advisors has been a bold step aimed at reversing this trend.

Changing scope of the need for evidence

Many uncertainties and challenges come from a rapidly changing demography, multi-faceted social change, globalisation, technology and the environment. There are continual challenges to the continuity of trends, relationships, and myths that have played a large part in informing and shaping past decisions. Such changes affect, for example, business form, wealth generation, and who make up the New Zealand of the future. Many of these uncertainties will eventually require a policy response necessitating making decisions with incomplete knowledge. Deferring decisions, in some cases, is likely to significantly reduce the welfare[52] of New Zealanders.

One explanation for uncertainty in policy response is that currently dominant research and analytical capabilities are based on an outmoded view of information, one in which there are low perceived benefits from network processes. Network processes are those that use appropriate analytical processes to exploit continuous streams of digital data to create information. The most well-known example of information extracted using network processes is the Google search engine.

The currently dominant research and analytical capabilities are suited to low velocity information. For example, case studies, however accurate in themselves, cannot form the basis of policy that will apply to large communities or the population as a whole, as they obscure the huge variation in the factors determining conditions and attitudes. New case studies for example, or different interpretations of them, have led to significant policy reversals, when policy has been formed on this basis. Case studies can highlight well how combinations of processes interact and hence highlight aspects of system performance that might otherwise go unnoticed except to the end consumer.

There are some widely adopted frameworks to report on conditions of society, economy and environment e.g. frameworks provided by United Nations, Organisation for Economic Cooperation and Development, and International Monetary Fund. United Nations conventions provide other reporting obligations. These and other legacy government information processes are often: small and fragmented; largely use data sources which are not subject to increasing benefits from network processes, involve high levels of manual intervention; and not accessible in a way which could fuel high velocity effects.

There are now available sources and methods that support network processes with effectively real-time information of high trust. Public policy information systems have been slow to invest in creating sources and methods to exploit the benefits from network processes. Applications that exploit network processes are: derived information, for example, the use of GST returns to assess the state of economic activity; content sharing, for example, student data to support applications for study and student loans; and content dissemination, for example, as was piloted in the United Kingdom Neighbourhood Statistics[53]. Each of these uses has increasing returns from automated and scalable processes which give increasing returns in the functional and operational processes used.

The development of the IDI has been a major step in this direction, although it is not clear that the analytical capability and capacity to challenge orthodox reasoning has advanced as fast as the computational capability. This has been supported to date by the leadership of Statistics New Zealand in the accumulation and integration of administrative records, the formation of an analytical group of statistical experts within The Treasury, and the creation of the Social Investment Agency.

The IDI provides rich opportunities to see the past transition pathways of targeted groups and identify where there have been concentrations of people with experiences that could be better supported with this new knowledge. The use in a protected environment of a confidential universal identifier has enabled the IDI to achieve a high level of integration across a wide range of government sectors and traditional sources including the census of population. This integration over time has built an evidence base that can examine individual transitions, concentrations of attributes and characteristics, and test causality. There are limitations in the IDI in its early stages as most of the information obtained from contributing departments did not conform to public sector wide standards as there were none, and documentation practices vary immensely across departments.

There is much that should be got from its use, and it is important to recognise that these administrative records are able to provide a rich retrospective view on the past performance of agencies and can inform potential improvements that have not been identified up to now. Much better knowledge can be uncovered about what did not happen when it should have. The IDI could also be used to identify significant cross-agency transactions that may be best managed by extending the responsibilities of agencies. Conceptually, the IDI is not about observing the actions of the state through the lens of the citizen. The experiences recorded by the state are specific to the statutory obligations placed on each evidence source and are quite unlikely to reflect the full experiences of citizens with the agency. Not all citizens are either included or comprehensively observed in the IDI. All evidence sources of populations have some practical limitations, and some conceptual ones. The lives of citizens are much more variable than can ever be captured by the information gathered in research models or in administrative data collections. Consumer perspectives and their full experiences need to come from other sources.

Information technology, particularly through the IDI, has added to the volume of evidence that can now be drawn on. There is a huge potential benefit from the effective management of the integration of disparate data sources. Longitudinal studies can bring an understanding of causality and rich insights about how behaviour and conditions might be influenced by particular interventions at a population, group or individual level. The IDI has expanded the information with which to estimate the likelihood of further engagement with social services by groups of individuals through linking records of individuals and facilitating analysis of the information of their experiences held within government agency records.

A foundation for government organisation formed from knowledge systems

Useful information is now readily available at low average cost from multiple sources[54], and the prospects are that this will improve even further. Government is now in a position to rethink its institutions on the basis of knowledge and available information, and dispense with a preoccupation with structure, conduct and a narrowed view of performance. This is not to suggest that government will become a metaphysical virtual enterprise, no longer engaged in providing physical services. Rather, the government's objectives can be achieved, for example, by setting standards of behaviour, collecting information on that behaviour, and where it is policy, by imposing sanctions for non-compliance. It is possible to contemplate customs, excise, and food safety objectives being realised in value networks with logistics systems based on effective and efficient information flows such as importing and exporting.

Government knows what it wishes to achieve and could use the operational information required to coordinate the value network but has incomplete knowledge of their working. For day-to-day operation, the value network is invisible and imposes little burden on participants. A lack of understanding of such networks leads to a misplaced confidence in 'command and control' managerial thinking, particularly in social services. As the range and intensity of many personalised social services increases, it is clear that more citizens could perceive a conflict between their relationship with a public agency able to sanction and penalise, and organisations in the community that they could have a long-term relationship with on complex personal matters where safety may play a part. The information needed by the state to work viably with such organisations is often crowded out by input focused controls and demand for access to individual citizen data.

What this says about the information on policy

What does this say about the capabilities required for the delivery of policy? Focus needs to be placed on knowledge of the entire value network in which the policy is to apply. Focus also needs to be placed on the lifecycle of the policy from its design, implementation and operation, through to its evaluation. Policy design should include the specification of: the information to be collected in order to assess its effectiveness; and the information gathering mechanisms to be used. Greater emphasis is required on operational systems and processes designed to facilitate the benefits from network processes. Process simplification and automated operational processes need to make use of digital information repositories to achieve increasing returns. Finally, there is an overarching need for clear statements of the purpose for collecting data from multiple sources, sound methodology, and access channels and conditions.

These capabilities point to a profound change to systems and processes which can require large investment and may involve high levels of dependency on information and communications technology, investment in the establishment and maintenance of metadata, and associated capabilities from, for example, data scientists and user experience designers. These factors make it difficult to justify new investment, and where it is justifiable, it is high risk.

Some government processes have sufficient scale to warrant this investment. Many do not because of the specialist services they provide. These problems can be countered by: integrating standard components; clubbing together with other agencies to use common systems and processes, for example of the type delivered as PAAS (digital information platform-as-a-service) solutions; adopting information architecture, standards and over time guide incremental change to the desired end state. These problems are no different from those faced by other types of organisations. The successful internet companies show that where this is possible, significant benefits are achievable and ineffective companies are replaced by more effective ones. This discipline does not apply to public sector organisations in the same way, so the sources of dynamism to drive public sector change needs to have a strong basis in citizen come-at-ability.

This problem is an ongoing one faced by the public sector and is exacerbated by technological change. It is endemic, and the solution lies in capacity to respond. The health system typifies the issues to be faced. On one hand, New Zealand has a well-managed nationwide service devolved to many sites which manage the collection storage and provision of blood, all of which are high risk activities. On the other, the selection of x-ray equipment and associated information exchange capability has long been a locally overseen activity, lacking a common exchange protocol that takes advantage of the information and communications technology available to the health system.

Much of the information on the conditions of society, economy and environment is framed to enable reliable international, time and geographic comparison. There is patchy coverage of information on the quality of public policy and the services they establish. Scientific methodology and deliberation has yet to evolve with the revolutionary change in the nature of data now being generated about our society, which appears to compete with rather than compliment legacy data collections. An information-based society needs new forms of investment that have yet to be decided on.

The breadth and velocity of circulation of information is a function of its perceived interest to those with access. Legacy government information systems and scientific information are not sources of high velocity information. New information and communications technology sources offer promise as sources of high velocity information, but also have limitations. Considerable opportunities exist to rethink public sector performance assessment, and the capacity to adapt services without resorting to the serial restructuring which has been the dominant response over recent decades.

"THERE, I KNEW WE'D FORGOTTEN SOMETHING! WE FORGOT TO CONTROL THE PIG."

Chapter 4

Increasing uncertainty and impact of conjecture

Obligation to report on society, economy and environment

Governments' responsibilities are many: to protect New Zealand's interests internationally, care for and develop its population, provide effective stewardship of resources, environment, rights and entitlements, ensure proper redress for criminal actions, and guard our future in ways that reflect our sense of place in the world. Information sources have not been organised to bring knowledge of the costs in total of these activities, or of the large share borne by citizens and business, current or future. All bring the obligation to report on their attainment by the public service, and to bring assurance that the authority to tax and otherwise oblige citizens has been properly and effectively drawn on to achieve this. The Statistics Act 1975 and Public Audit Act 2001 support this.

The recognition and balancing of tensions between places, generations, cultures, sectors and social groups is informed by the quality of, insight and foresight made possible by the range of evidence that can be regarded as trustworthy by all relevant communities. Some of the responsibilities of governments such as child protection and reducing violent crime involve long-term commitments that can stretch analytical, fiscal and managerial capabilities in the face of divergent public sentiment and understanding.

The likely origin of easily accessed information sources can be global, national or local. The internet, global media, and the new social media extend the multinational reach of information sources. A strong feature of information sources selected in this way is that they are slanted towards sources that have a strong 'human interest' irrespective of the veracity of that source. Even where the information source has integrity, standing is often given by the inclusion of a contrary view under the guise of balance reporting, where the two views are not of comparable standing. This failing is frequently seen in media reporting.

The trustworthiness of evidence used in policy analysis is dependent on the knowledge assets that can be drawn on. Vital for sound policy analysis is an understanding of how the natural variability of the population is reflected in the representativeness of the information on which policy is based. The trustworthiness of information will be based on it having some mix of the following characteristics: realism of measures; awareness of representativeness; depth of quality assessment; continuous evaluation; demonstrable trustworthiness of methodology and research design; transparency of judgments implicit in methodology; information on the nature of the variability of the represented populations, and the detection and management of the influence of outliers; and challenge from other sources of information.

Tension between government action and impact

There is a need to balance the difficult tensions between making timely decisions and basing decisions on sound information, as well as recognising the part of conjecture in informing policy options. The preparedness of the public, business and not-for-profit agencies, the public service and politicians to accept uncertainties in the effectiveness of government policies provides the context for this tension. Many situations require decisions where knowledge is incomplete, for example about the severity of the consequences of inaction or delaying decisions (such as delaying the age of entitlement for superannuation[55]). At such times, the authority to act needs to be accompanied by indirectly associated knowledge, and the ability to judge the relevance of associations with tangible evidence elsewhere.

The most solid determinant of such a capability is experience, a past capacity to anticipate and identify scenarios for which contingencies can be prepared in advance, and the capacity to engage with resources not usually associated with the processes, that have more knowledge of rare situations (e.g. international emergency teams) with an immediacy that reflects the consequences for human life and health. Acquiring knowledge from relevant experience can itself be a highly-structured process, exemplified by apprenticeship schemes as are still seen in medical training.

Understanding how far to invest in such capability in advance of any problems arising is difficult to assess except by those with rich knowledge of the sector, and the ability to understand the alternative ways by which problems can be framed. Contemporary performance assessment processes, either of institutional capability, executive and leadership potential in the sector, and general management development philosophies often undermine rather than enhance this capability.

A well-functioning economy and justice system, along with a well-functioning education and health system increase resilience to adverse pressures and events and bring continuous learning opportunities. There will always remain uncertainties about the scale, location, timing and duration of the next rare adverse but not totally unexpected event, such as an earthquake, oil spillage, tsunami, pandemic or plane crash. For many of these, mitigating action taken in advance, and the effectiveness of immediate leadership will have dramatic impacts on the capacity to minimise loss and recover. With short-term time horizons, finding resources for contingencies is often crowded out, and this was most obvious in the years following the changes to public sector management in the late 1980s. Compounding this, some key public agencies have continued to dilute their knowledge base through serial restructuring.

Whether change is in response to slowly evolving or dramatic situations, there needs to be an understanding of when and how to make sound decisions that are trustworthy. Future policy responses are weakened, and hence the opportunity cost from deferring decisions rises, when the need to invest in the means to recognise and reduce the uncertainties faced is significantly downplayed. The need to highlight such uncertainties may well test the robustness of the constitutional underpinnings of government. Deferring policy change inevitably reduces the range of policy options and increases the share of the electorate which judges such change as electorally unpalatable. Where decisions are deferred in such situations, typically this may be only until a crisis arrives. The growth over the last two decades of policy specific advocacy groups, the internet and talkback radio, frequent opinion polling alongside MMP have all made Ministers quite rapidly aware of shifts in the balance of public sentiment, generally increasing the likelihood of unpalatable but necessary policy responses being delayed.

Another important source of inertia within the public sector comes from individuals or groups who may not support change and use a variety of tactics to delay. Management will give priority to those change initiatives which will easiest deliver a net benefit. This latent inertia in maintaining low value activities, can in our view, be a perverse outcome of the strong 'stewardship' culture in a public sector focused on maintaining and preserving current functions and their associated activities.

In a small country such as New Zealand, where the public sector comprises a comparatively large share of activity, trustworthiness and trusted decision-making processes need to be particularly important characteristics. This is because of the small scale of open, informed, objective challenge to the recognised wisdom of the nature of government, society and commerce. In addition, a demonstrable capacity to reason needs to be competent to address the nature of the issues faced by governments. Without this, few means exist for independent assurance that trustworthy decisions have been taken on behalf of citizens, and that assessment of the effectiveness of the capacity for bringing effective outcomes to otherwise irreconcilable tensions of time, generation, place and sector interests has occurred. Such assessment mechanisms would have some features of continuous improvement, many to show that due process has been followed, and many will need to provide evidence after the event.

The limited resources available also mean that there are constraints on the role that can be deployed by government. The consequence of resource limitations starts with the unavailability of the skills to deal with all important issues. There has been little investment in the resources available to provide information to citizens to build understanding of key issues. This extends to the size and depth of the independent media able to analyse and comment on complex issues. Given that many of the major policy responses of executive government are rarely final, there is only limited recognition of the likelihood of revisiting policy choices, and the potential contribution from improving information sources prior to this[56].

Tension between global competitiveness and procedural purity

There are weak mechanisms to challenge the accountability of the public sector when thinking about the poor performance from the public sector as a whole or as a network system. There is a plethora of mechanisms to monitor compliance with procedures, delivery of outputs and performance of individuals and single agencies, especially chief executives. Close scrutiny of compliance with procedures, output delivery and individual performance does not and cannot inform or assess the performance of the system as a whole, and completely fails to consider the information needed to assess any of the forms of deadweight losses, and to manage their reduction. The Better Public Services programme may not have changed this to any marked extent.

The institutional arrangements that now exist allow the executive government of the day, of Ministers and their departments, to govern with the greatest degree of freedom. No government of the day is expected to reduce this freedom and is more likely to be motivated to further increase the freedom to make decisions. One extremely serious constitutional disadvantage of this freedom is that there is insufficient responsibility to oversee an effective and efficient public sector, as well as to best use the wealth of the nation in generating wealth for the future in the best interests of current and future citizens. The desperate state of crowding in prisons are examples of these limitations[57].

Where effective and efficient policy options are available, and public sector performance is demonstrably effective, then there is a higher likelihood that difficult, politically unpalatable choices will be taken by Ministers. This is challenged by an increased emphasis on ongoing opinion polling, a media focus on failure and the trivial or irrelevant, the emphasis on failure by the Parliamentary opposition, and limited think pieces on long-term public issues that can capture the public stage (we contrast this especially with the reports issued by 'research institutes' and consultancies which engage in advocacy). This provides ministers with many disincentives that prevent publishing evaluation studies or sustaining institutions that bring alternative thinking.

This matters because of the significant impact of the public sector on national income generation. There are strong external forces acting on New Zealand to lower growth, compared to countries which are less isolated and more effectively part of larger regional groupings[58]. For example, other small developed nations such as Ireland, Norway, Sweden, Czech Republic, Slovakia and Slovenia, to which New Zealand is frequently compared, are part of the large European Union regional grouping. Sub-optimal public sector performance costs all New Zealanders by way of reduced national income generation.

The preparedness for change that is an essential concomitant of continuous improvement is seriously impeded by the political context of the public sector. Change may be delayed until a crisis generates a political constituency for action. This is particularly the case when inadequately funded organisations obscure problems in addressing major social, economic and environmental issues. The Expert Review of the Child, Youth and Family Agency of Ministry of Social Development highlighted the consequences of funding tensions that were generally invisible through the regular departmental accountability framework[59]. To be effective, the public sector management system needs to be able to function well despite a very constrained context. This deficiency can be seen in the difficulty of governments to make some long-term policy decisions, e.g. superannuation.

Poor information limits policy options, especially when public sentiment is a strong influence on the political acceptability of choices. New Zealand is one of the most violent of the Organisation for Economic Cooperation and Development countries. Highly visible violent events necessitate a political response, and in the absence of sound research most policy innovation involves adding penalties or sanctions, leading to New Zealand having very high incarceration rates. Being tough on crime is important electorally, making redistributive justice and long-term thinking difficult, especially where a long history of denial of important causative factors such as child abuse lingers on. For some 50 years, we have known that Māori have entered custodial institutions at rates of up to eight times that of Pakeha, with little abatement despite falling crime rates[60].

What this says about the information on building the capacity of society, economy and environment

Policy as determined by Ministers needs to be the result of a balance that is struck between the values of society and the evidence base that assesses the viability of policy, as well as other tests of fairness, including international conventions and rights legislation. How evidence challenges and informs values will be reflected in decision-making processes.

While a party's manifesto sets out its priorities these are modified by coalition agreements and the need to get legislation passed. The limited supporting policy information provided is crafted so as to promote the government's position. The election manifestos have reduced in importance as accountability documents since the mid-1980s. The size of New Zealand makes it unsurprising that anecdote and sentiment can determine how the government applies and invests in information and makes visible its reliability. The recent report by the Chief Science Advisor[61] to the Prime Minister on the Justice system and imprisonment is one of the few vehicles currently to challenge this pattern.

Information and Institutions of Government Accountability

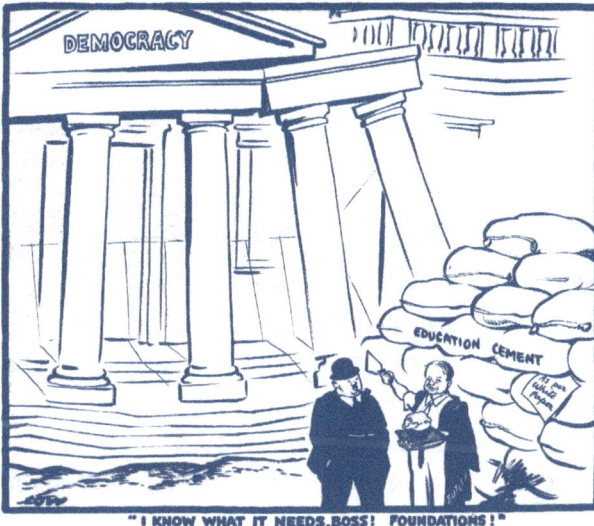

DEMOCRACY

EDUCATION CEMENT

"I KNOW WHAT IT NEEDS, BOSS! FOUNDATIONS!"

Chapter 5
Information as part of the system of government

Balancing the different arms of government

Our central propositions are that government should be seen as a system requiring information and capabilities to ensure that its purposes are realised. In the complex setting in which government operates appropriately rich information needs to be collected and disseminated. Information for this purpose is required for each function of government. This chapter looks at these information requirements, and how the forms and quality of evidence can differ across sectors.

The rule of law recognises that the separation of the making of laws from their execution is a key protection to ensure the trustworthiness of governments, and that governments are able to be held to account through the capacity for open, informed and objective challenge. There are many ways by which the public might have assurance that good decisions are made by government. The conduct of Parliamentary business under the Speaker of the House, the Standing Orders and Parliamentary Question Time are important to this.

Public assurance is promoted by defining in legislation how government business will be conducted with sufficient credibility that it will withstand public scrutiny and assessment by Parliament. For example, the fiscal responsibility obligations of the Public Finance Act 1989 set out the processes which apply to the financing of government and public expenditure, and the appropriation processes and accountability to Parliament for spending, upon which the Treasury is required to report.

Sound policy is usually based on a testable understanding of context, and capacity to reason appropriate to the issue. Public assurance is promoted by enabling enquiry of any sort to be initiated by the legislature, of any action of government, and supporting such enquiry by officers of Parliament such as the C&AG. For example, through the C&AG citizens can potentially obtain assurance that those who hold responsibility in the state have accountability for their financial actions, regardless of their autonomy, election or appointment process. This is reinforced by having autonomous and properly funded officers of Parliament who report to Parliament rather than government. They have the capacity to make public any assessment of matters within their purview resulting from the concerns of citizens. However, Parliament places strict rules around the behaviour of its officers, for example, by convention the C&AG does not comment on government policy.

For the appointed public service, the obligation to be held to account comes from: departmental statutes, Public Finance Act 1989, State Sector Act 1988 and the Official Information Act 1982. There are also various governance mechanisms, including the Cabinet Manual, responsibilities to a specified Minister, collegial support mechanisms provided by the

State Services Commission with personal development and promotion pathways, external reviews and commentary by the media and non-governmental institutions.

For governments, the authority to act brings the obligation to explain, and be thoughtfully challenged. The obligations for providing the evidence to enable this to occur are dealt with in the Official Information Act 1982. The focus of these is on process integrity rather than the effectiveness of Parliament in advancing the wellbeing of its citizens.

The need to stand again for re-election (for elected MPs) or endorsement of the party (for list MPs) cannot in itself be sufficient vindication of the decisions made by Cabinet Ministers, nor can it be the conferment of unfettered authority. This is not only because many decisions have impacts far beyond the three-yearly electoral cycle, but because the high opportunity cost from deferring adjustment to policies will usually be unknown, and often unrecognised. Few manifesto commitments can be considered as genuine choices for the electorate, given that it is often Ministers alone who have determined the extent of public awareness of the effectiveness of their own decisions. Having said this, obligations exist under the Official Information Act 1982 and these empower commentary by the media and non-governmental institutions. Not all government organisations tend to be well informed on matters of concern to them whereas the media have an overriding imperative to provide coverage which is newsworthy.

The managerial processes operated by the public sector are also important to enable the public to have assurance that good decisions will be made. These include processes that maintain an independent public service appointed on merit relevant to the job[62], so that properly qualified people are placed in leadership and professional posts, posts that place high expectations of personal integrity on appointees. Sound practices define and require clear standards of ethical behaviour, and appropriate accreditation of any required competence, while the state also must be a good employer. The public service is expected to be an exemplar in employment equity and human rights.

Operational performance

Operational capabilities implementing and supporting government policies function under a complex set of conditions, all of which modify their effectiveness and efficiency. The accumulation of experience in managing any of these conditions usually results in formalising procedures to enable more effective response in the future. Without review processes, such procedures can lose relevance over time, and impede rather than enhance efficiency. The relationship between Ministers and chief executives can obscure the accountability for doing this, where short term exposure of faults might result.

The public sector reforms of the 1980s provided a much-needed lift in the integrity of the public finance system, making it possible to define more clearly (and often limit) the role of the public service agencies, and required Ministers to be explicit about their expectations. The reforms also engineered opportunity for innovation and flexibility in practice although after just one decade this was increasingly followed by a heightened political aversion to risk taking in operational matters. Service integration between public agencies narrowed rather than increased as the complexity of the population and their needs widened. The 'no surprises' principle has resulted in limits to innovation, evaluation and explanation, by the consequential actions of Ministers and their departments. It is not unusual when issues arise that require a response relevant to long-term stewardship, for official responses to be preceded by efforts to diminish the importance of the original concern, especially when it brings more immediate embarrassment or challenge. Housing, imprisonment, child protection, Māori redress and water quality present many examples of this occurring. In almost all situations, it is the challenge to those usually responsible by an external source that results in government being held to account.

Some of the ways of practically managing such tensions include formalising conventions and clarifying decision-making responsibility and processes for response. The drinking water quality fiasco at Havelock North pointed to a need for systematising how to inform the public with great immediacy when the town water had become contaminated. Secondly, internal decision-making processes needed to reflect the urgency for speed in this, while testing procedures needed to be properly informed by potentially predictable changes in the uncertainty about water quality. All these were lacking in Havelock North[63] at the time.

Risk management planning can be oversimplified by ignoring events, such as those that have a low chance of occurring but whose high impact can be significantly mitigated by precautionary action. When dealing with rare events, the ability to accumulate and apply knowledge from the past and from others in similar situations is dependent on how experience is accumulated and protected. The preference now in the public sector is for people with general purpose management skills, but their limited knowledge of the technical specifics of the function being managed and high turnover has reduced the means of protecting the knowledge gained from experiences of rare events. For example, the recent earthquakes in Christchurch and Wellington have changed earthquake awareness (because of its recency) but not necessarily the oversight of other types of rare events. Nor has there seemed to be significant transfer of knowhow from the plethora of other rare events to the development of a systematic capacity to learn, instead, each is treated as a separate on-off occurrence.

Integrating elements of government systems

For each distinct functional system within government, and for the system of government itself, the central elements of network management must be incorporated into the roles and structures of the authority needed for public service-wide and sector-specific leadership (including: systems leadership; information; system, processes and standards;

and the right skills and knowhow). These elements need to fit the circumstances of a small, highly dispersed population, and prevent the loss of economies of scale and scope that fragmentation will otherwise bring. Information for this purpose is broad-ranging and includes sources from: knowledge centres; the capacity to know what happens now; accumulating experience of what works elsewhere and within the system itself; performance monitoring information relevant to the goals of government; and information on managed linkages and connections between the component systems of government. Recognition in roles and structures of the authority needed for public service wide and sector-specific systems leadership also covers: relevant all-of-government systems; synergy between official and political processes of executive government advice, decision-making and implementation (Cabinet); managed investment of State resources; providing citizens with opportunities to give or withdraw trust in the functions of government; well-founded culture and ethics of public service; and effective government institutions.

A particularly serious failure since the 1980s reforms of public management has been the dominance of narrow self-referencing measures of performance focused on elements of process and distant goals rather than citizen experiences. The autonomy of individual agencies has seriously constrained the potential for cross-agency network leadership and the operational cohesion that determines the quality of citizens' experiences with public services. The poor support and general lack of interest in Whanau Ora with government departments also reflects both the extent of cultural change needed[64] and a general disinterest in network system innovation. A well-functioning networked system will have continuous improvement as a central element of its managerial ethos, and monitoring service failures extensively in support of its focus on consumer satisfaction.

What this says about the information on government performance

Government must manage the tension between: its relevance as a complex system operating in a dynamic environment; and applying consistent practices to ensure that it can be trusted to do this. Information for this purpose needs to be appropriate to the issues of the times and the consideration of future generations. Instead, most information on government's performance is provided in fiscal terms to enable the nation to be seen to be comparable to peers. The way in which serious deterioration of the buildings of the Counties Manukau District Health Board was disclosed highlights the vital importance of contextual information, and process that binds Ministers, Parliament, boards and public servants into the same level of integrity of reporting[65].

Accountability founded on the trustworthiness of intelligently designed systems that help people place and refuse trust intelligently has four implications for the information provided by government to facilitate come-at-ability. First, it requires information that can be understood by people so that it empowers intelligent decision-making. Second, the scope of the information, on the one hand, should enable the citizen and their communities of interest to see themselves in the information. On the other hand, the information should be evidence of the trustworthiness of the systems and processes of the functions of government. Third, the need for government to provide this information should not be time-bound and should place no obligation on the citizen to continually monitor and sieve through information provided by government. The information should be available, accessible and intelligible when the citizen and their communities of interest have a need for it.

SPEEDWAY MODEL

Chapter 6
Information to intelligently place and refuse trust

Placing trust

By the end of the 1890s the evolution of New Zealand as a nation had set the state on the path as a highly-trusted contributor to the welfare of its Pakeha citizens, while it continued as the coloniser of Māori. For Pakeha, that trust in the state limited the need for oversight mechanisms to justify what led them to decide on the 'good works' that they did. Over the following century, the rights of Māori were eventually acknowledged, and some redress began.

The state has progressively become more intrusive, as a regulator, screener of eligibility and deliverer of sanctions, and the state can no longer rely on its very involvement as sufficient justification for what it does. The capacity of citizens to enquire, and the expectation of an answer, continues to grow. The emerging place of the Courts in this, and the appointment of Ombudsman, the passing of the Official Information Act 1982 and then appointing independent Parliamentary Commissioners have been periodic responses to assure trust in government. The arrival of MMP has shifted the way that citizens influence policy, although the expectation for mechanisms to assure trust appears to have grown.

The presumption on the part of government that citizens will readily make decisions to place their trust in the institutions of state and the services provided by and on behalf of those institutions can no longer be assumed to hold. This chapter investigates the role of information in the ability to hold government to account and the forms information takes to make loss of trust less likely. Limitations on the ability of individuals to place and refuse trust intelligently are due to the opacity surrounding many operational elements of government.

Trust has many foundations. Faith in a religious, political or social cause may bring confidence in actions and conditions without the need for evidence from experience of any sort. Evidence from experience may come from the assumptions that arise from the accumulated experiences of others, perhaps gathered scientifically and founded on an appropriate scientific analysis of the evidence. How people balance available evidence alongside the direction pointed to by values has yet to be fully acknowledged as fundamental to the society we have become[66]. Key to trust is the reliability of the information itself on which trust is based, in the context of the values of the society. Being able to judge the integrity of the information source is vital where the information is expected to challenge the values of society, or significant communities within society. The validation of trust needs to reflect the extent to which such policies and programmes justified by the information reflect the values of society: otherwise failures are likely to have consequences for trust in the policy and government itself. Without transparency in the limitations of what can be based on available evidence, the extent to which trust in policies and programmes is based on conjecture will be hidden from citizens. The delivery of the policies may be based on flawed assumptions about the characteristics and conditions of those screened for eligibility with resulting impacts on the effectiveness, efficacy and cost of any programmes that are put in place.

Independent mechanisms to hold government to account

The strongest of mechanisms that assure trustworthiness are constitutional safeguards, such as the requirement to have general elections every three years (if not earlier). At other levels of government, the mechanisms are much weaker. There are also some long established obligatory processes:

- Electoral boundaries are set every five years immediately after a census of population by a committee of independent officials and political party representatives, in a process whose integrity is unlike that known to be used in any other country
- The Judicial system, including its specialised Courts for Families, Youth, Environment and Employment
- The Waitangi Tribunal
- The Ombudsman
- Coroners Courts
- The Official Information Act 1982
- Trust in the payments by the state to those who are appointed through a political process is managed by the establishment of an independent body, the Remuneration Authority.

Other mechanisms to deal with poor quality of service and which require institutional responses include the Independent Police Complaints Authority, The Health and Disability Commissioner, the Children's Commissioner, Taxation Review Authority, Privacy Commissioner and the Human Rights Commission. Meeting obligations under international conventions such as the United Nations Convention against Torture have been the justification by the Ombudsman and Children's Commissioner to enable them to inspect prisons and youth detention centres.

Of significance for trust, is the manner with which day-to-day transactions of public agencies are carried out. For those who deal the most with these agencies, respect is reportedly highly variable, while for those with complex issues, the quality of connection between different entities, even of the same agency, seems to depend primarily on the capacity and endurance of the citizen rather than the design and integration of the processes of public administration. Where there have been new mechanisms, evidence of trustworthiness can emerge only after long lead-times.

The Waitangi Tribunal set up in 1975 is an extra-ordinary example of the way in which a high level of transparency, even belatedly, can lead to recognition and partial rectification of wrongs of great significance to the whole population.

Misplaced trust

Over time, in most of the distinct systems of government examples can be found where trust in government has been revealed to be seriously misplaced – even by the standards of the day. In such situations, the earnestness of efforts to understand, provide redress and learn can reinforce trustworthiness rather than diminish it while attempts to escape genuine discovery may compound the loss of trust.

The cost of misplaced trust should not be underestimated. A number of examples have already been mentioned, but there are other examples that have been less visible, such as attitudes of sexism in the Police and Military, and ethnic bias in application of discretion of authority. And still to be fully understood, are the impacts on the public of screening practices that have become invisible through purportedly commercially sensitive algorithms that currently lack proper validation and oversight[67].

Through social media, one-off situations in one place, however isolated and rare, can become a tangible part of the evidence base available to all, anywhere around the globe. Evidence of trustworthiness may be formed from just one personal experience, or of the reported experiences of others. As long as the provenance of information is not taken into account, there can be some evidence in support of almost any proposition, and there are many examples where robust scientific evidence has wrongly faced challenge from an unusual situation that may be un-replicable[68].

Unlike the Police, Taxation, the Intelligence Services and other parts of the state sector that have statutory authority over some activity of citizens, in the social services and corrections there is no embedded system of judicial review by citizens about their individual cases, and on some matters judicial review has been prevented by statute. The increased targeting of programmes places a continually growing share of citizens under the obligation of means or income testing through agencies where heightened security or reaction to difficult situations has resulted in the physical environment becoming increasingly unfriendly. The recent Court decision following the murder in Ashburton of two Ministry for Social Development staff saw the Judge[69] decide that greater protection of staff was needed in these sorts of offices. This brought to the fore the difficulties in such service organisations in balancing the safety of staff and the quality of interaction between staff and beneficiaries. The court case highlighted how these can be weighed up differently by politicians, the judiciary, regulatory bodies and public servants, generally at a cost to citizens who visit the premises for services.

The strong legacy presumption on the part of government that its institutions should be trusted by reason of their existence alone is manifested in: an absence of independent oversight mechanisms being provided to challenge the quality of service. This makes the coordination of multiple services difficult and results in poor follow up when evidence is inconsistent with intended practice, leading to avoidance of judicial review of decisions.

Independent processes that belatedly have been put in place for holding agencies to account after some highly visible failing are costly and may require citizens to challenge the state before anything happens. For example, there were public calls for an independent enquiry into the 1979 Erebus air disaster, irrespective of the enquiry by the government regulatory agency (the Civil Aviation Authority), with this second enquiry reaching radically different conclusions as it looked more widely at all aspects of the accident[70]. More recently, citizens have called for an inquiry into the current issues faced by victims of past cases of child molestation in the care of the Child and Young Persons Service[71]. The current review body up to 2018 has been the government department that was responsible for the failings, the Ministry for Social Development. As another example, in November 2017 the Supreme Court judged that the Solicitor-General erred in deciding not to prosecute the managers of the Pike River mine, in an appeal taken to the Court by grieving families[72].

To complicate matters when enabling people to intelligently place or refuse trust, governments in recent decades have been much more responsive to withdrawing government provision of services from areas which can be supplied by the private sector e.g. road construction and prison services. In areas where government has applied its resources to deliver services, it has had great difficulty doing this in a consistent coordinated manner e.g. services to at-risk families. In addition, inconsistency in the application of processes has generated high costs for users of government services through high compliance costs and weakness in process improvement practice. The operation of social services does not appear to take cognisance of the high likelihood and potential high rate of screening errors, as exemplified by the Housing Corporation testing of methamphetamine residue in rental houses[73]. In child protection services, there has been a difficult balance between the allocation of resources to screening new notifications, and for the care and support of children already in care. In the past, the balance may have shifted in response to particular incidents, rather than any analytically based knowledge of risk.

Development of trust can be undermined by attempts at a political level to measure and manage processes through tight controls on communications, including the application of Cabinet's 'no surprises' principle. Such approaches sidestep the fundamental attribute of being able to place trust, and they instead assume a momentary delineation of risk, often narrowed to embrace the reputation and volubility of the political executive of the day. Because past institutional performance tends to frame the plethora of monitoring and assessment mechanisms within the public sector, system management failures are generally poorly prepared for. Where systems are recognised at the highest levels as not functioning well, the almost certain presumption is of institutional or executive failure, rather than of a need to gain a deeper understanding of the context.

The operation of child protection services, reducing family violence and recidivism are areas where government responses have not been based on an understanding of the long-term dynamics prior to policy change. These are situations where there is weak evidence of being able to hold government to account, and where Ministers and public servants have acted with inadequate justification. Many of the tasks undertaken by public services, including child protection, imprisonment, responding to family violence or treating the consequences of severe mental health problems are highly challenging, often functioning with partial information and operating within organisational structures better fitted for earlier times. Drug use, pornography, violence and continual social change are just a few causes that bring an ever-evolving context to these roles.

For the public and politicians, sentiment and the right to voice opinions on any matter hold sway. This is irrespective of their veracity and the public mind displays asymmetry of attitudes about establishing the accuracy of these. There are tensions at times between the rationalist view of the high use value of scientific information and public sentiment. An example is public health information and acceptance of scientific information by the public. An illustration of this is the measles/mumps/rubella (MMR) immunisation, where the science shows the public benefit of immunisation to be overwhelming, yet there is only an 83 percent immunisation rate, where the level required to prevent an outbreak is 95 percent. The issues here are that people who choose not to inoculate children are putting at risk the lives of people who cannot be or are not yet fully inoculated. These susceptible people rely on protection provided by the rest of society[74]. This applies also to the formulation of public policy which is unsupported by scientific information[75].

Part of the reason for this tension is that scientific information is often incomplete, and at time may be incompatible with prevailing myths and stories – many of them supported by personal anecdotes. Even where there is the intention for policy decisions to be evidence based, with democratic political processes it is not always possible to reach agreement on what those policies should be. More often, measures of uncertainty in scientific estimates are undermined by comparisons by commentators in which counter arguments are based on drawing generalised conclusions from specific exceptions or anecdotes.

While executive government must balance many potentially irreconcilable tensions of time, place, generation and sector, for delivery purposes it has chosen to split the functions of government across a wide array of departments and agencies, few of which have the same perspective on these tensions, so political judgement, in the end always must be exercised – reinforcing the view of the dominance of political judgement.

From a practical perspective, it is increasingly likely that the functions in which government takes an interest will not be contained within the responsibilities of any single government agency (at least, as they now operate). Many social services involve organisations and people outside government. In an attempt to overcome this deficiency in the accountability structure, outcomes have been devised, and sometimes several entities will contribute to the attainment of an outcome. But this mechanism cannot disguise the fact that: first, performance of government that is most critical to chief executive assessment is based on the outputs and fiscal constraints contained within entities rather than across them. Second, even where policy integration occurs at a national level, operational integration across public sector organisations is much more likely at a local level, particularly under conditions of constrained budgets. Third, in some cases effort toward local integration occurs without national level integration or support. The recent Integrated Service Response[76] pilots regarding family violence highlight significant gains for family safety in collaboration and responsiveness, but they also highlight the high cost at present of such co-ordination. This pilot has wider implications across other sectors, because of its approach to cross agency collaboration and its impact in an area of social services where poor collaboration can have a huge cost to those involved.

For very good reasons, the Justice sector consists of organisations that have distinct places in our system of government, providing fewer levers for integrated responses than other parts of the state. The Judiciary, Police, Corrections Department and Parole Boards are expected to have a high degree of independence in their operation and practices. Each of these component bodies tends to focus on solutions that they can manage, so that Corrections for example tends to focus on the prison stock, prison operations and other offender programmes. Consequently, any government-wide strategy to significantly reduce offender numbers and prisoners needs to be explicitly comprehensive and include initiatives particularly fitted for each of the Judiciary, Police, Corrections and Parole Boards, as well as the wider social services sector. The accountability regime based on performance measurement applied at a department level, as well as fiscal oversight and the sector wide specification of outcomes is simply inadequate for holding government to account in such a complex sector.

Across the state sector, agencies are expected to lead effectively in issues that have major importance to economic performance and social wellbeing. Essential ingredients of this include strong Ministerial collaboration, sound system-wide governance, clear insightful outcomes, and analysis, insight and capacity for debate. Typical of the policy issues represented here include financing, transport, water and energy infrastructures, location of national services such as higher education and tertiary health, court processes, environment, species protection, rehabilitation, workforce planning, services providing protection from harm, and national control of strategic assets. Of particular concern are issues where the state must act as guarantor of last resort. Examples already discussed include leaky homes, earthquake recovery and Treaty claims, another example is banking stability[77].

Once elected, Ministers work with a public service dedicated to advise and implement public policy, but who are unevenly prepared for analysis and evaluation, and generally weak at network leadership and thinking. Since the introduction of MMP in 1996, to form a government, there has been a need for the rapid acceptance or rejection among potential coalition partners, of policy shifts and initiatives that can bring together a majority of MPs and hence the formation of a government. To be effective in the 'hot-house' of post-election negotiations, ideally all political parties should have had ongoing access to the best research available. Instead, these discussions risk having to endorse policy founded on anecdote and myth, because of the limited material about critical public issues that is usually available to opposition parties or the limited resources to analyse the available information (or even the limited interest in performing rigorous analysis). A rich knowledge base does not fit with popularist politics.

In a democratic political system, the party processes for policy making are another impediment in the use of scientific information in political decision-making. Campaigning on their manifesto, elected political parties are to some extent bound by them, but to a much lesser extent than occurred before the introduction of MMP. While there is some room for a new government to modify policies on the basis of what is learned on taking office, moving away from the manifesto still requires political courage. Recent general elections have shown that the modification of election promises by the new governing political party come about even more quickly.

Intelligently not placing trust in government

Objective evidence of the untrustworthiness of government can lead to decisions by people to behave accordingly. In extreme cases, citizens have been able to refuse participation with the agents of government through civil disobedience e.g. 1978 Bastion Point protests, and 1981 Anti-Springbok tour protests. At a constitutional level, freedom of speech and assembly are legitimate forms of protest.

Decisions not to place trust in particular institutions of government and specific public services are more difficult and there are no mechanisms to measure the extent to which this is occurring. Even where there is evidence of completely inappropriate actions by government there has been a reluctance to respond other than at an elevated, institutional level e.g. Cave Creek platform collapse[78].

Various mechanisms are used by people to withdraw trust from the various branches of government. The decision not to vote is one of the responses to a loss of trustworthiness. Challenges to Government can take the form of court action of unlawful limitations on individual's freedom of speech, association, protest and detention; complaints to the C&AG, and non-enrolment for elections. Challenges to the judicial branch of government include: failure to pay fines and civil disobedience at court decisions; continued appealing of decisions of lower courts; and flight from the country. The Pike River case referred to earlier is an example of the Courts being trusted more than the public service. The executive branch of government can be challenged in many ways including: non-participation in civic duties (such as the Census and jury service) and voluntary activities (such as school boards and donating blood);

opposition to government programmes (such as public health initiatives); and use of alternatives (for example, private health care and education).

Despite a duty of care for the provision of its services to mitigate the impact the possibility of misplaced trust, there is a noticeable absence of information and mechanisms to enable people to intelligibly place and withdraw trust in government. It is also noticeable that this information vacuum is filled by private and non-governmental agencies, for example, social commentary in the media from the regular reports on social services by the Salvation Army, or the occasional study by the Auckland City Mission.

Trust incorrectly withheld

A situation of particular concern is where trust is withheld mistakenly. This situation is readily seen in low support at times for public health campaigns such as immunisation where the scientific evidence is erroneously discounted. In some instances, misleading information is disseminated to further the agenda of a group of stakeholders (e.g. smoking and effluent pollution of waterways[79]).

Failure to give proper recognition of when trust in government is well founded

Given the backdrop of recognised instances of government failures or suspicions of failure (e.g. the spying of government agencies on New Zealand citizens[80]), it is increasingly difficult with the existence of social media for successful government initiatives to gain the credit they are due when trust in government is well founded, for example the public health programmes such as fluoridation, smoking, and the public housing programme. Taking one of these examples, the public housing programme, introduced as far back as the Workers' Dwelling Act 1905, arguably made a major contribution to building the capacity of society, economy and environment, but that contribution is often not well understood.

As the state increases its capacity to connect the information it has about citizens, there is a risk that the state may over-penalise individuals when they challenge the state in one domain, by extending enforcement action to other domains, outside the oversight of any judicial authority. Examples are drivers licence loss after non-payment of fines, and reparation taken by the Ministry for Social Development from future benefit entitlements rather than as part of Court decisions[81]. There is currently a private members Bill[82] in Parliament to take away welfare benefits from those who do not comply with community sentences.

Even where information is collected it may not portray the true impact. It is known that for social services involved in protecting people from harm, reporting rates often mean that half or more of people involved do not wish to depend on or trust the service. Surveys of secondary pupils point to just 51 percent of girls who have been abused sexually having reported this to anyone, and the corresponding result for boys in the same situation is 72 percent[83]. The ongoing Australian Royal Commission into sexual abuse in institutions in Australia found a mean lag of 22 years between abuse and first reporting it among those it met[84].

New Zealand does not calculate take up rates for the populations eligible for social services and benefits, but if they were regularly available they would indicate trends in trust. The willingness to respond to the census is perhaps our richest source of variation in compliance among age, ethnic and other groups in New Zealand.

Until recent decades reporting domestic violence would not have resulted in the extent of police action that now occurs. It is now recognised that to protect all in a family from such harm, a much deeper understanding of situations is needed when first responders arrive at violent domestic events.

Citizens need objective and trustworthy information about the nature and condition of society, including population, economy and environment, so that progress can be assessed, and questions of importance determined and highlighted not only by legislators, but by the media and others in public life. This is another facet of processes operated by the public sector, particularly where this facilitates subjecting advice provided to government to the scrutiny of expert peers in national and international forums.

Coming-at government for inadequate public services

Citizen come-at-ability can be facilitated by first, providing the channels to challenge decisions, at policy and operational levels. Second, citizen come-at-ability is facilitated through the provision of information and the forms in which it is made available. A third approach to facilitating citizen come-at-ability is to increase knowledge of issues, for example, through education and awareness programmes (such as on retirement provision). A fourth approach arises where the government establishes processes which independently initiate review. The Coroners Court is one such mechanism, as are the Health Quality Death Review Committees. In tax and policing as well as official statistics, New Zealand has high compliance rates by international standards, and both taxation and policing decisions are subject to independent judicial review by standing bodies.

Measures of uncertainty provide a rich source of information in assessing policy options, and also in the design of processes, structures and standards, as well as performance measures. Raising understanding about the nature of uncertainties and risks, and how they are taken account of in decisions would be a natural concomitant of this. It would enable a greater capacity to establish whether failures in performance reflected the mix of likely outcomes from an imprecise process, or system failure. The Parole Board exists to decide when an imprisoned person can return to normal life and the conditions that they will be expected to meet. If there were zero acceptance of re-offending, then some imprisoned people would experience longer and possibly indefinite periods of incarceration, as absolute certainty is well-nigh impossible in such judgements.

For improving policy choices, more knowledge that can reduce the uncertainties of the future would assess the deadweight loss from executive government poorly responding to such uncertainties and enable the impact on communities of citizens to be assessed. The information provided would need to include a suite of information of the state of selected aspects of society and the economy – these are national statistics. This approach could be augmented by incorporating commissioned research of selected topics such as the impact of climate change. The scope of information provision could be made even wider to provide access to all government information.

As the velocity of circulation of information of all sorts increases, especially that of personal anecdotes of experiences, it seems likely that this task will become harder in all societies, and perhaps more so, the smaller the society is.

What this says about the information to enable the intelligent placing and refusing of trust

In general, there is little done in public services to design functions with the ability to place and refuse trust in that function – this means that there is poor come-at-ability. Come-at-ability provides the ability of a citizen, through their and their communities of interests' experiences, to be empowered to hold government to account for the timeliness, quality and quantity of those experiences. This empowerment comes from the ability for a citizen to see herself and himself, and their communities of interest in the data provided by the state. Where those mechanisms exist, then it would appear to reduce the chance that trustworthiness will be questioned, by what is becoming an increasingly powerful use of social media. Ironically, much less information is provided in areas where there is a high volume of transactions. In these areas, reduced trust can have unforeseen consequences, and it is social media that have expanded the range of these volatile areas.

Chapter 7

The importance of information to hold government to account

A mechanism to improve government accountability

The current set of arrangements instils a high degree of trustworthiness in key democratic processes, but these arrangements are not particularly good at helping individuals to place and refuse trust intelligently, in the government of the day and its policies, or in public institutions and their services. This can result in a gradual decline in trust in government itself, and a reduced belief in the importance of traditional processes to shape how and what it does and for whom.

The trust of citizens in constitutional and institutional arrangements is moderated by the day-to-day relationships of government with its citizens and the quality of its policy decisions. There are clear processes which have to be followed in statute. Some processes are administered by public servants who have a statutory authority to impose sanctions and penalties without judicial oversight. At the highest level of decision-making, the governance and management arrangements embodied in the institutional and operational structures are designed and operate to give effect to the decisions of Cabinet and Ministers, with few mechanisms to challenge them. One consequence of this is that policy risk is high because of limited deliberation, and the limited mechanisms to challenge and test the efficacy of policy decisions. The knowledge base of government is impaired by a weak regard for significant knowable trends and weak mechanisms for government to obtain free and frank advice.

Significant opacity surrounds operational elements which are uneven in performance with instances of areas requiring significant improvement. Both the poor commitment to connectedness and the fragmentation of the public services into many small agencies add to the difficulties citizens have in forming a view on outcome attainment from their experiences and from available performance measures. Where it occurs, system integration across agencies is more reliant on Ministerial direction, rather than strengths in managing complex delivery systems and processes. Government response to addressing family violence exemplifies this well. There is a strong culture of compliance with agency process. For those delivering services this means that they are slow to respond to change. The change that does occur can lead, at a political level, to the artificial enhancement of a position which generally accompanies limiting evaluation and improvement processes and obscuring of past performance.

The most well researched and informed programmes are to a degree experimental, as knowledge about the issue, the population it affects, the policy responses and the capacity to put the policy in place as it is designed are all likely to be partial and continually changing. Policy formulation involves the exercise of choices, some of which may not align simply with the empirical evidence available, especially as the evidence that is available for policy decision-making may be insufficient, incomplete or ambiguous. This has been demonstrated by the British Government's dismissal of Professor Nutt as scientific advisor to the Advisory Council on the Misuse of Drugs after comments he made about the government's illicit drug policy[85]. In New Zealand it is more likely for a Minister to have to leave their post because of a matter of probity, rather than capability.

Even in situations where there are deficiencies in information, sound policy needs to result from trustworthy and informed judgments and decisions, which then form the basis of effective action, action both to initiate new policy, or to refine and even repeal ineffective policy.

To achieve this necessitates a capability to analyse the nature of the issues faced by governments, as well as the ability of the system to demonstrate that trustworthy decisions have been taken. There is also the requirement to reconcile tensions amongst time, region and sectorial interests. In the absence of information, research and insight, it is myths, ideology and anecdotes that are likely to determine key elements of public programmes, and substitute slogans for policy analysis. Examples of slogans are: "Three strikes and you are out", "No kid left behind", "Tough on crime, tough on the causes of crime" and "A billion trees". Where this does not occur, a strong evidence base of a range of forms is essential to ensure integrity in institutions, relationships and systems, and coherence and impartiality in the decision-making at an operational level.

Government bears unnecessary high intangible costs because of the predominance of serial structural change internal to the organisations that make up the public service. Changes to the machinery of government, where new agencies are created, or existing agencies combined, are comparatively rare. Such restructuring has the intent of moulding the purpose, priorities and direction of the agency by the necessity to accommodate shifts in the way particular regional, national and international communities are recognised. What is generally underestimated is the consequential loss of connection at many levels of the restructured agency with other parts of the sector that they participate in, and the connections of citizens and their organisations, both commercial and community, to them. The levers that governments have to manage, in the face of significant shifts in both the context of government and the pressures on it, are the capacity to deliberate, a government's effectiveness in its capacity to act and to manage the quality of delivery, and to ensure the relevance of the means of accountability. At Ministerial level, the potential capacity to drive connectedness is both strong but sparing and diminishes at operational levels.

Key elements on the information of government in New Zealand

The concept of government in New Zealand as a knowledge centre founded on the effective leadership of a wide range of sources of evidence is poorly developed. This is the case even where the capacity to provide information has always played a central role. The burden of being an independent arbiter of the information needed to hold government to account falls separately on the C&AG, Government Statistician, the Judiciary and some special purpose bodies including the Royal Society. The current set of essentially ad hoc arrangements and some enduring components does not underpin a high degree of trustworthiness in government, and it is not particularly good at helping individuals place and refuse trust intelligently. Developments are ad hoc, and in the face of the rise in alternative media, they are unlikely to maintain or increase citizen perceptions of the trustworthiness of public management. The nature and scale of emerging privacy, equity, personal protection and human rights issues make understanding the place of information and how evidence is obtained and used a matter of deepening importance.

The information base at its best provides for the oversight of the operation of the constitutional system; and the place of the citizen with respect to the political processes of public administration. For example, the electorate and election processes are robust. Financial reporting to Parliament is well established. There is less, largely ad hoc, information on: constitutional restraints on the executive; access to judicial processes and quality of public services.

On most of the other key issues faced by government, there is insufficient systematic information produced. There are significant limitations in the institutionalised mechanisms and on the uses of the information that is potentially available. Mechanisms where stakeholders can provide feedback, which are a key part of continuous learning practices, are almost non-existent or ineffectual, as are evidence-based policy formulation processes that are founded on drawing comprehensively on the evidence that could have been accumulated. There are examples where successful major change interventions have been put in place, and it is noticeable that these information systems have good accountability mechanisms. Successful change initiatives are less likely to occur in the face of the risks of the new information age, without recognition that the most vital competence of a public sector is thinking about future information needs and practices, and how that is led.

While considerable resources are dedicated to the production of evidence of agency efficiency and fiscal prudence, assessing this needs a deep understanding of the place of various types of evidence. The nature of the performance measures that dominate public accountability narrow attention to particular results. These results gain prominence to enable the government of the day to define how it seeks to have its achievements framed and measured, and its agencies assessed. Reliance on these measures has led to a narrow understanding among Ministers and public officials as to the level of trust on public services and government generally. While 'Good to Great' is periodically revived as a leadership mantra of the public sector, difficult problems remain so, and long-term resolution of inter-generational concerns continue to evade us. Alongside this is the unrecognised amount of speculation in the knowledge base of all policies.

Where the knowledge base is thin, then sanctions and penalties are well used options that reflect our history as a punitive society. There is almost no knowledge of the impact of sanctions and penalties. In many areas, penalties have become significant tools (such as institutionalising children and adults) and there is only anecdotal and small study information on the effects, but they generally point to perverse[86] effects that may have end results far worse than the original event which led to the sanction. Sanctions and penalties are a poor and possibly counterproductive substitute for well-designed accountability processes. They are often not impartial in their impact. Those who administer penalties need to be subject to unambiguous processes by which they can be held to account, given the many situations of abuses occurring when independent oversight is poor or non-existent.

In a small democracy with limited resources the deadweight cost of the inadequate information to hold the Government to account is high. It is difficult to assess the cost and depth of impact of poor government decisions on the capacity, resourcefulness and resilience of society, economy and environment. In public services, monitoring of failures can generate discoverable records that embarrass, compared to the benefits of continuous improvement with its simplicity and ease of their application. As a counterweight to undue influences, citizens need effective mechanisms to intelligently place and refuse trust in government, not only in the election of the government of the day and its policies, but also in the public institutions and the services that are an ongoing part of government.

The ability of citizens to come-at government

At a constitutional level, the information provided to Parliament describes the resources available to Government, how those resources were intended to be used, how they were applied, and the probity of the processes followed in using those resources. Governments also provide selected evidence to demonstrate their achievement in delivering their election promises. There is a high degree of trust in these institutional processes of government. The same conclusion cannot be drawn for the ability of a citizen to assess the impact of a Government on the wellbeing of the nation. The three-year election cycle is the mechanism available to citizens to guide their aspirations. The information provided by Parliament is poorly suited to enabling citizens to vote intelligently.

Outside of the accountability mechanisms to support a Westminster Parliamentary system, there is no coherent systems-thinking view on the information of government. Public relations departments of the agencies of state might explain what government policies are, but do not provide information that led to the formulation of these policies, how these policies are to be assessed and the actual performance. Nor are mechanisms provided for citizens to interact with government by withdrawing trust from public service where there are systemic failures.

The consequences are seen in policies which will not in their current form reflect the future context that ought to be revealed by the informed foresight that already exists, and which others may have. This is relevant for environment protection, climate change, income inequality, retirement provision, offender management, violence or child protection, in particular.

The general presumption that competitive market services supplied by alternative providers will deliver a means by which government can be held to account requires informed markets which are unusual in the social services – most particularly for service provided on a statutory basis. Furthermore, punitive actions exist for 'clients' that fall foul of the service prescriptions, even where these can be the consequence of deficiencies in government policies, systems and processes. The mechanisms to withdraw trust in government are simply not up to the task of service improvement and development.

The coherence, relevance and trustworthiness of the information that the state gathers about itself to enable citizens to trust how government serves them now, is needed to prepare a better future for later generations. Such information to empower come-at-ability is rare. Social media have added a new and significant factor in how people can determine whether or not they perceive a trusted basis for particular policy choices based on anecdote and one-off personal experience – views that have no systematic foundation. Comparable technological shifts have created opportunities to lift the analytical support for policies. Unless the come-at-ability of citizens as recipients of programmes of any sort is recognised as a vital element of service provision, more information could well increase uncertainty, rather than reduce accountability and oversight.

How information is prepared and used to hold government to account is vital for the health of a democratic society. What makes it vital for this to be managed explicitly and coherently is that the very apparatus of the state that is being held to account has prime responsibility for enabling the monitoring for this to take place. State apparatus is indispensable for information management in a democracy. A germane example of this is the determination of electoral boundaries. The processes by which governments get elected determine, and are determined by, perceptions held by citizens of the legitimacy of government actions. Integral to these is information and how it is applied to the determination of electoral boundaries, and the processes of identifying and engaging electors. This has been done in a most trustworthy manner, unlike many countries that we might otherwise admire for the strength of their democratic foundations.

New Zealand's Parliaments have put in place a narrowed set of performance measures and requirements to follow specified processes, as mechanisms to hold government to account, for example, the requirement to publish budgets and audited financial statements. The set of information government makes use of for decision-making is also an important element of democratic accountability. It informs how the various interests of its many types of communities are balanced, the interests of future generations are recognised and how the rule of law is maintained. When it comes to the actual effectiveness of policy interventions and the operational performance of public services little systematic information is provided to enable citizens and their communities of interest to meaningfully hold government to account.

It is important to acknowledge that government needs to act on behalf of citizens in a multiplicity of diverse situations, often with less information at the time than could have been available if decisions were able to be well anticipated. In addition, it is not possible to anticipate or codify all the forms of information that are material to monitoring the multiplicity of ongoing and one-off situations that may vary in stability, observability and measurability.

Evidence to hold government to account takes many forms, and much may be of unknown and perhaps unknowable quality. Whatever form information takes, there needs to be ways of learning about its comparative validity and reliability in the context of other information sources. Nonetheless, there needs to be assurance that no particular form of information is privileged so that others are ignored, not collected, or even dismissed or obfuscated. This is not always apparent from the stated intention of providing the information. For instance, the focus on agency-specific performance measures leads to indicators that are easy to measure and advance the government's agenda, downplaying the importance of monitoring the experiences of citizens in using public services. The focus on outcomes can dilute attention given to the quality of inputs.

While the context of this discussion is central government, the comments are also relevant for local government and crown entities. The incidents with the Havelock North town drinking water point to a narrowing of the perceived purpose of those involved, as the maintenance of the flow of water seems to have diminished the paramount necessity of protecting the public health of citizens.

Similarly, making policy decisions by matching recent and past performance, because the data is readily available, has negatively impacted on the adaptability and innovative capability of many public services[87]. Furthermore, not considering the consequences of uncertainty in policy analysis results in unjustified confidence in that policy, and the programmes and the rules and processes that are adopted to implement the policy. These deficiencies in policy analysis have been highlighted in past policies to support children and youth[88]. The reality is that inherent in all policy and programme administration is uncertainty of some form, and that should be made explicit.

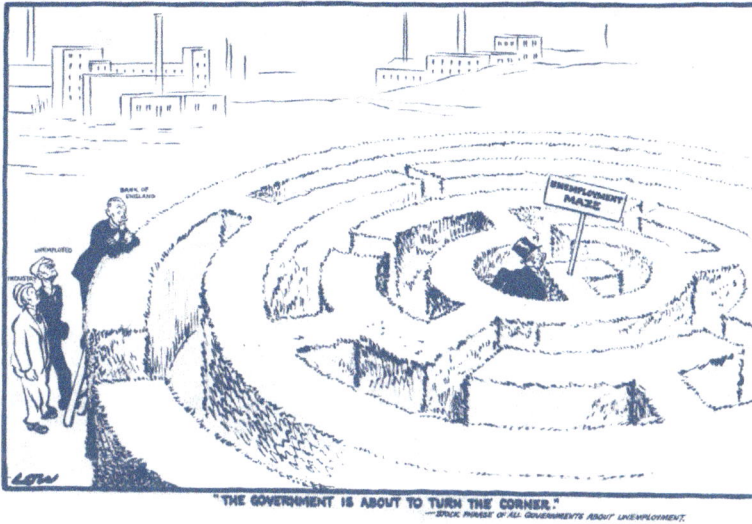

"THE GOVERNMENT IS ABOUT TO TURN THE CORNER."
—STOCK PHRASE OF ALL GOVERNMENTS ABOUT UNEMPLOYMENT.

Chapter 8
The makings of a path ahead

We have shown that there is no comprehensive government-wide concept of information and supporting capabilities to hold government to account. Fiscal management is the only area in which comprehensive information is provided by government, and that can be undermined by pressure not to report the impact of financial restraint, for example on asset depreciation or service quality. In all other aspects of government performance that span policies, building capacity of society, economy and environment, performance and placing and refusing of trust in public provided or funded services, the available information is uneven or non-existent. This is especially relevant today, with significant shifts in the communities of interest and the weight given to different forms of information.

There will always be consequences of a poor ability to hold government and its agencies to account, sometimes occurring very much later. These negative consequences include: the reduced public authority of key referees including Judiciary, C&AG and Government Statistician; loss of trust in government agencies and perhaps government more generally; poor decisions on the range of solutions that agencies believe they need to institute; and poor estimation of the certainty of the worthwhileness of their work. A poor ability to hold government to account may also contribute to the declining propensity to vote[89].

While governments may seek to control the agenda of what messages are conveyed to citizens and other stakeholders, it is another matter to deny the preparation and use of relevant information. Understanding Māori dispossession, disability, measuring poverty levels, gender equality of opportunities and counting unpaid activity have all belatedly become matters of government accountability. This has happened despite major impediments by those more concerned with the nature of consequent action than the information itself.

In making the case for a systematised oversight of information capabilities through which citizens hold government to account we also recognise that events and crises form natural experiments that can enrich understanding that can be applied wherever relevant. For example, the failure of storm water systems in South Dunedin in 2015[90] highlights so many multiple points of operational failure that they might be expected to impact on how those operating all such systems are held to account in the future. In the same way, a forensic analysis of what in the past enabled child abuse to be prevalent in public institutions intended to protect children may have considerable relevance in the better protection of those in the custody of the State now.

Government information management also needs to be cognisant that there are cultural differences in the way people judge that they have been able to hold government to account. This is not only in the form of accountability and means of engagement, but in determining the relative importance of issues, and in the ability to withdraw trust in government. The diversity, mobility and variety of New Zealand's peoples increasingly typify New Zealand society in all its population centres. Institutions that have narrowly codified society in ways that have been fundamental to the past shape of policy are less able to serve current citizens through existing practices. As an example, marriage, the nuclear family, home ownership and life-long male employment are no longer such dominant characteristics that they typify the New Zealand household.

The Treaty of Waitangi places many obligations on the Crown, but it is the Crown that shapes the information needed to hold the Crown to account, and there is as yet little consideration of how the decisions of the Crown can be challenged by Māori as a matter of process rather than protest.

The very existence of government information generates a duty of care on government to respond deliberately to what the evidence shows, even if the eventual conclusion is to ignore it. The more trustworthy the information, the more government must recognise the consequences of the information on the actions of others as well as its own. For example, while local or central government may choose to ignore evidence of liquefaction risk or sea level change from global warming, insurers will probably not, with possibly serious consequences for the underwriting of the Earthquake Commission.

If we are not well prepared for the present, we will be in an even less relevant state for a future where scrutiny can only grow, as the place of the individual anecdote about experiences is magnified in the knowledge base, and the importance of an impartial information referee to counteract this grows. The users of services will always know more about service failure and the counterfactual to sound performance, and this needs to be harnessed and put in context to support continuous learning processes.

There are already areas of policy, such as offender management and tests of eligibility for welfare benefits, where without a well-functioning information capability to hold government to account, citizens can react to the complexities of society by selecting political options which reject the multifaceted character of society in favour of a perceived simple set of slogan policies. The absence of such capabilities provides challenges for the public authority of the C&AG, Government Statistician and Judiciary to remain impartial information referees in order to maintain the confidence of society in government. Without such capabilities, the preparation and release of important evidence by the public sector can depend on the relationship between Ministers and the public service, as set by the characteristics, experience and style of individual department heads, rather than by well-established conventions and other transparent obligations that apply to all.

Having the confidence and competence to make rigorous and systematic use of the mix of the available forms of information relevant to holding government to account would be the foundation for more informed foresight about the future context. This contributes to the formulation of better policies and ensures operational competence and impartiality no matter how the underpinning policies are determined.

Constitutional arrangements enable the executive and Parliament to make and change rules to get things done. The counterweight to this dexterity in decision-making is sufficient relevant information to empower the citizen to come-at the state. Such information needs to reflect 'me and my communities of interest'. Failure to empower citizens to come-at government brings risks of fragmenting society.

A start to the creation of such information could be made by three initiatives. First, a regular independent review and reporting of the state of information supplied. Second, institution of formal, independent oversight of mechanisms by which functions of government are come-at-able by citizens. The institution of formal, independent oversight of mechanisms by which functions of government are come-at-able by citizens would require agencies to provide for external scrutiny of how they gather evidence to assure themselves of the 'standard to which those primary tasks and obligations are discharged'[91]. This would include independent mechanisms for the trustworthiness of services. Third, ensuring the continued relevance of mechanisms to build and retain public trust in information gathering and exchange. All government functions need to be required to provide appropriate support to the above three items.

As part of a regular independent review and reporting of the state of information supplied, there would need to be a regular assessment of the available scientific capability in evaluation, research methods and foresight. The key characteristics of a coherent information system to hold government to account can be summarised into four distinct elements spanning: the government scientific capabilities (covering for example Statistics New Zealand, government analytical centres, and Royal Society); external validation of the trustworthiness of services as provided by judicial processes, Royal Commissions, the Ombudsman, and independent public inquiries; public engagement and information exchange (a wide ranging set of arrangements covering information policy, accessibility to evidence, ethical practices and cultural recognition and relevance); and leadership of social, economic and environmental services delivery, innovation, evaluation, and structure.

Policy and services that influence the social, economic and environmental condition and progress of the distinct communities and generations that make up our society need to be justified with information that has distinct relevance to them. The particular political, cultural and constitutional positions of these communities need to be reflected in the many sources of information that inform the state and hence its citizens. We have identified the key elements of this, and the makings of a path ahead.

Notes

1   Often cited as a comment attributed to Adolphe Quetelet, Belgian statistician (1796–1874).

2   For example: Closer Economic Relations Trade Agreement between Australia and New Zealand; Australia, New Zealand, United States Security Treaty; and Comprehensive and Progressive Agreement for Trans-Pacific Partnership.

3   One exception was the review of child protection, which led to the reformation of CYPS into Oranga Tamariki. *Family Violence Death Review Committee, Family Violence Death Review Committee Fifth Annual Report,* Health Quality & Safety Commission, Wellington, 2016.

4   A notable instance where systematic value-for-money evaluation is carried out is in the funding of state highway projects. For a description of this framework see New Zealand Transport Agency, 2015-18 NLTP Investment Assessment Framework – Overview, *New Zealand Transport Agency* [website], 31 January 2017, www.pikb.co.nzassessment-framework/2015-18-nltp-investment-assessment-framework-overview/, accessed 30 April 2018.

5   The firefighting foam contamination of airports is an example of this, for a timeline of the background to this see Radio New Zealand, 'New Zealand firefighting foam investigation: a timeline', *Radio New Zealand* [website], 10 April 2018, www.radionz.co.nz/news/national/354590/new-zealand-firefighting-foam-investigation-a-timeline, accessed 30 April 2018.

6   Controller and Auditor-General, *Ministry of Education: managing support for students with high special educational needs,* Office of the Controller and Auditor-General, Wellington, 2009.

7   As an example, the new Minister's announcement soon after taking office of the establishment of a new department to manage re-entry into the Pike River mine, the Pike River Recovery Agency, within the Ministry of Business, Innovation and Employment. See A. Little, 'Pike River Recovery Agency Established', *New Zealand Government* [website], 20 November 2017, www.beehive.govt.nz/release/pike-river-recovery-agency-established, 30 April 2018.

8   State Service Commission, 'Better Public Services: Results for New Zealanders', *State Service Commission* [website], 13 March 2107, www.ssc.govt.nz/bps-results-for-nzers, accessed 30 April 2018.

9   S. Elias, 'Managing Criminal Justice', *Criminal Bar Association Conference,* Auckland University Business School, Auckland, 5 August 2017.

10 The IDI is a database operated by Statistics New Zealand containing linked data is about people's life events such as education, income, benefits, migration, justice, and health, as well as the Census of Population. The data comes from Statistics New Zealand surveys, government agencies and non-government organisations. Linked to the IDI through tax data is the Longitudinal Business

Database with detailed data about businesses. For more detail see: Statistics New Zealand, 'Integrated Data Infrastructure', *Statistics New Zealand* [website], 20 February 2018, www.stats.govt.nz/integrated-data/integrated-data-infrastructure/, accessed 30 April 2018.

11 Cabinet Office, *Cabinet Manual 2107*, Department of the Prime Minister and Cabinet, Wellington, 2017. Section 3.22 explains: 'The style of the relationship and frequency of contact between Minister and department will develop according to the Minister's personal preference. The following guidance may be helpful. (a) In their relationship with Ministers, officials should be guided by a "no surprises" principle. They should inform Ministers promptly of matters of significance within their portfolio responsibilities, particularly where these matters may be controversial or may become the subject of public debate.'

12 'The public interest has many facets, and it would be deplorable if the assessment of the public interest were to become the exclusive province of the executive itself. Secrecy and security have to be balanced against the legitimate demands for an informed public opinion which is, when all is said and done, the essential element in a country which claims to be democratic.' D. Williams, *Not in the Public Interest*, Hutchinson & Co, London, 1965, p 216. Cited by S. Elias, 'Administrative Law for "Living People"', *The Cambridge Law Journal*, vol. 68, no. 1, 2009, pp. 47–66, p54.

13 H. Rutherford, 'NZ First's Shane Jones wants ministers to have more power over public sector', *Stuff* [website], 2018, www.stuff.co.nz/business/103382755/nz-firsts-shane-jones-wants-ministers-to-have-more-power-over-public-sector, accessed 30 April 2018.

14 An example of successive government limiting information is the issue of child poverty in New Zealand. See for example M. Dale, M. O'Brien & S. St John, *Left Further Behind: How Policies Fail the Poorest Children in New Zealand*, Child Poverty Action Group, Auckland, 2011, and more recently L. Cook, Submission on the Child Poverty Reduction Bill, Social Policy Evaluation and Research Unit, Wellington, 2018.

15 In this case the Ministers Bennett, Tolley and Adams over the period from 2014 until 2017.

16 O. O'Neill, 'Holding Accountability to Account', *Royal Statistical Society Beveridge Lecture*, Royal Statistical Society, London, 2009.

17 Leaky homes have been a disastrous consequence for houses, schools, prisons and hospitals and resulted from a weakening of standards of building materials, and light-handed management of regulation and inspection obligations. For detail on the background to the regulatory failure see B. Easton, 'Regulatory lessons from the leaky home experience', *Policy Quarterly* [online], Vol. 6, no. 2, 2018.

18 The Modernising Child, Youth and Family Panel, *Investing in New Zealand's Children and their Families*, by Ministry of Social Development, Wellington, 2015.

19 The offices of Ombudsman, the Law Commission and the Children's Commissioner have observed this formally.

20 The findings of the review of public policy advice (G. Scott, P. Duignan & P. Faulkner, Improving the Quality and Value of Policy Advice, The Treasury, Wellington, 2010) and the disdain with which the insufficiently researched Task Force 2025 was received, signal major inadequacies in the capacity for effective deliberation of policy. For a recent presentation on the cost of poor policy-making which results from insufficient use of sound evidence in government see P. Gluckman, *The role of evidence in policy formation and implementation: A report from the Prime Minister's Chief Science Advisor,* Office of the Prime Minister's Science Advisory Committee, Auckland, 2013.

21 J. Due, 'The New Zealand Goods and Services (Value-Added) Tax – A Model for Other Counties', *Canadian Tax Journal,* vol. 36, no. 1, 1988. Cited by A. Maples & A. Sawyer, Adrian, 'The New Zealand GST and its Global Impact: 30 Years On' *New Zealand Journal of Taxation Law and Policy.* No. 23, 2017, pp. 9-26.

22 PricewaterhouseCoopers, *Weathertightness – Estimating the Cost,* Department of Building and Housing, Wellington, 2009.

23 In a 2013 deal aimed at saving 800 jobs in the southernmost town of Bluff after New Zealand Aluminium Smelters threatened to move offshore, a lengthy standoff was ended with a $30 million Government subsid. See P. Smellie, 'Tiwai Pt smelter safe to Jan 2017 under new Meridian deal', *NBR* [website], 8 August 2013, www.nbr.co.nz/article/tiwai-pt-smelter-safe-jan-2017-under-new-meridian-deal-wb-143996, accessed 30 April 2018. A 2017 view of the role of subsidising the Tiwai Point smelter provided by the Electricity Regulator is reported by P. Smellie, 'Electivity regulator sees long future for Tiwai Point smelter', *NBR* [website], www.nbr.co.nz/article/electricity-regulator-sees-long-future-tiwai-point-smelter-b-209442, accessed 30 April 2018.

24 There are many examples where public-sector officials have imposed on society economically hazardous policies with the underlaying presumption that people and businesses who participate in the area covered by the policy do so at their own risk without explaining those risks in advance e.g. deregulation of the building industry (B. Morris, 'Leak crisis will hit every pocket'. *The New Zealand Herald* [website], 2 July 2011, www.nzherald.co.nz/nz/news/article.cfm?c_id=1&objectid=10735864, accessed 30 April 2018) and the Emissions Trading Scheme (R. Hughes & P. Molloy, 'Is the ETS worth the carbon it is written on for small-scale forest owners', *New Zealand Journal of Forestry,* vol. 61, no.4, 2017, pp. 33–36).

25 This is discussed by O'Neill, 'Holding Accountability to Account'.

26 Introduced in: A. King, *The British Constitution,* Oxford University Press, Oxford, 2007, to describe the accountability of government to the public through a clear line of sight to someone responsible.

27 An example of this is the matter of the severe degradation of building in the Counties Manukau District Health Board, described by J. Moir, 'Middlemore

Hospital: What really went down between health minister and Counties Manukau DHB?', *Stuff* [website], 24 April 2018, www.stuff.co.nz/national/health/103249836/middlemore-hospital-what-really-went-down-between-health-minister-and-counties-manukau-dhb, accessed 30 April 2018.

28 For example, some biological risks such as tracking the movement of livestock in the Mycoplasma outbreak because of inadequate compliance with animal tagging (G. Hutching, 'Farmers given ultimatum to comply with animal tagging system', *Stuff* [website], 20 December 2017, www.stuff.co.nz/business/farming/100059267/farmers-given-ultimatum-to-comply-with-animal-tagging-system, accessed 30 April 2018).

29 Selling off state houses while homelessness was well into a decade long upwards trend. See A. Johnson, P. Howden-Chapman & S. Eaqub, *A Stocktake of New Zealand's Housing,* New Zealand Government, Wellington, 2018.

30 Providing a state funded supplement to house rentals may have led to the predominance of houses being bought as rental properties in Otara, rather than for home ownership, contributing to the downward spiral in Pacific house overcrowding and rental expenditure rising as a share of income for the poorest.

31 When one of the authors was appointed Government Statistician from 1992, the then Minister of Statistics told him that he "needed to have the same assurance in the integrity of the Department of Statistics when he got into opposition as he expected to have as Minister".

32 The establishment of the Reserve Bank Act 1989 made the Reserve Bank responsible for independent management of monetary policy to maintain price stability.

33 In June 2017 there were 311.4 FTE communications professions employed in the public sector. State Services Commission, *Capping the Size of Core Government Administration, 30 June 2017 Update,* State Services Commission, Wellington, 2017.

34 In the face of criticism about failures in the performance of emergency services in responding to natural disasters, including the 2011 Christchurch earthquake, and other emergencies a Ministerial Review commenced in June 2017 (Department of the Prime Minister and Cabinet, 'Ministerial Review: Better Responses to Natural Disasters and Other Emergencies in New Zealand', *Department of the Prime Minister and Cabinet* [website], 18 June 2018, www.dpmc.govt.nz/our-business-units/ministry-civil-defence-emergency-management/ministerial-review-better-responses, accessed 30 April 2018.

35 Anne Tolley, Minister of Social Development (2014-2017) refused to conduct an inquiry into historical abuse of children while in the care of the state despite the early findings of an Australian Royal Commission and evidence of the prevalence of abuse and its impact on Māori children from the Confidential Listening and Assistance Service chaired by Judge Carolyn Henwood, *Final Report of the Confidential Listening and Assistance Service 2015,* Confidential Listening and Assistance Service, Wellington, 2015.

36 Such as population and social change, loss of employment opportunities, technological innovation.

37 A common practice in public policy development is commission a range of narrow focused, consultant reports. For some consultancies, writing these reports for various government agencies is their main activity.

38 For examples, the Confidential Listening and Assistance Service (C. Henwood, 'Carolyn Henwood: Time has come for New Zealanders to clearly state how children should be treated', *Stuff* [website], 13 February 2107, www.stuff.co.nz/national/89359350/carolyn-henwood-time-has-come-for-new-zealanders-to-clearly-state-how-children-should-be-treated?cid=facebook.post.89359350, accessed 30 April 2018.), and the Ministerial Committee of the Inquiry into Violence led by Justice Roper (G. Newbold, *Crime, law and Justice in New Zealand*, Routledge, New York, 2016,p 106).

39 Family Violence Death Review Committee, *Family Violence Death Review Committee Fifth Annual Report.*

40 Ministry of Justice, Regulatory Impact Statement Bail Amendment Bill, *Ministry of Justice* [website], n.d., www.justice.govt.nz/assets/Documents/Publications/Regulatory-Impact-Statement-Review-of-aspects-of-the-bail-system.pdf, accessed 30 April 2018. The Regulatory Impact statement for the Bail Amendment Act 2013 asserted that some 45 to 50 additional prisoners would result. Currently the final impact is estimated at 1,500.

41 Hon Bill English, Minister of Finance (2008–2016).

42 New Zealand Productivity Commission, *More Effective Social Services,* New Zealand Productivity Commission, Wellington, 2015.

43 The Modernising Child, Youth and Family Panel, *Investing in New Zealand's Children and their Families.*

44 It is our observation that this is seen in the downward trend in publishing internal evaluation studies by social sector Ministries, in the face of a strengthened commitment by Ministers for evidence-based policy.

45 A view which the Head of the Department of Prime Minister and Cabinet has indicated he wishes to challenge. A. Kibblewhite, *Mastering the art of free and frank advice*, Speech to IPANZ, 17 August 2016.

46 Ministry of Justice, 'Regulatory Impact Statement Bail Amendment Bill', *Ministry of Justice* [website], n.d., www.justice.govt.nz/assets/Documents/Publications/Regulatory-Impact-Statement-Review-of-aspects-of-the-bail-system.pdf, accessed 30 April 2018.

47 S. Elias, 'Fundamentals: a constitutional conversation', *Harkness Henry Lecture 2011,* University of Waikato, Hamilton, 12 September 2011, p 9.

48 John Key's off the cuff but undeliverable commitment regarding those killed in the Pike River mining tragedy is an example (D. Cheng & A. Bennet, 'Pike River mine: NZ a nation in mourning – Key', *New Zealand Herald* [website], 25 November 2010,

www.nzherald.co.nz/nz/news/article.cfm?c_id=1&objectid=10689944, accessed
30 April 2018).

49 M. Cropp, 'Researchers can predict 3 year olds' future problems', *Radio New Zealand*
[website], 13 December 2016, www.radionz.co.nz/news/national/320246/
researchers-can-predict-3-year-olds'-future-problems, accessed 30 April 2018.

50 D. Preston, *For Whom the Bell Tolls -The sustainability of public social research
institutions in New Zealand,* Social Policy Evaluation and Research Unit,
Wellington, 2018.

51 The Treasury, *Review of Expenditure on Policy Advice,* The Treasury, Wellington, 2010.

52 Professor Sir Nick Stern in his analysis of global warming assessed the cost of
prolonged inaction, in a way that has much relevance to many other areas of
public policy. For background on this see for example: The Economist, 'Stern
warning', *The Economist* [website], 2 November 2006, www.economist.com/
node/8108221, accessed 30 April 2018.

53 For a description of the Neighbourhood Statistics project see: Office for National
Statistics, 'Neighbourhood Statistics – Focusing on Local Statistics', *Advisory Group
Paper AG(02)16,* NeSS Data Development Programme, Office for National
Statistics, London, 2002.

54 Although the capital investment is high, and in many cases increasing.

55 J. Edens, 'A guide to NZ Superannuation – what you need to know, and why', *Stuff*
[website], 6 March 2017, www.stuff.co.nz/business/money/90087663/a-guide-to-
nz-superannuation--what-you-need-to-know-and-why, accessed 30 April 2017.

56 The report by the Periodic Report Group, *Retirement Income Report: Interim Report,*
Periodic Report Group, Wellington, 1997, was unusual in that it set an agenda for
improving the information base for its final report. The group was disbanded by
the Labour government of 1999-2008.

57 P. Gluckman, *Using Evidence to Build a Better Justice System: The challenge of
Rising Prison Costs,* Office of the Prime Minister's Science Advisory Committee,
Auckland, 2018.

58 P. McCann, 'Regional economic development: Analysis and planning strategy',
Regional Science, Wiley Blackwell, vol. 88, no. 3, pp. 696-697, 2009.

59 The Modernising Child, Youth and Family Panel, *Investing in New Zealand's Children
and their Families.*

60 A. Donnell and R. Lovell, *How Many Offend?,* Research Report No 7, Department
of Social Welfare, Wellington, 1982.

61 Gluckman, *Using Evidence to Build a Better Justice System: The Challenge of Rising
Prison Costs.*

62 One significant benefit of having a competent public service is that elected
representatives can be selected from the whole population, not just those equipped
to analyse, develop, and evaluate policy and administer complex programmes.

63 Government Inquiry into Havelock North Drinking Water, *Report of the Havelock North Drinking Water Inquiry: Stage 2,* Department of Internal Affairs, 2017.

64 'But Whānau Ora cannot work unless mainstream well-funded government agencies become more accountable, more transparent and perform. One of the biggest problems in New Zealand is that we believe in a historical well-performed public service Reality is, there is no such thing as a public service anymore – that went out with Rogernomics' (J. Tamihere, Government agencies must become more accountable – Tamihere, *Stuff* [website], www.stuff.co.nz/auckland/local-news/western-leader/98420048/government-agencies-must-become-more-accountable--tamihere, November 2017, accessed 30 April 2018).

65 J. Moir, Middlemore Hospital: 'What really went down between health minister and Counties Manukau DHB?', *Stuff* [website], www.stuff.co.nz/national/health/103249836/middlemore-hospital-what-really-went-down-between-health-minister-and-counties-manukau-dhb, accessed 30 April 2018.

66 Gluckman, *The role of evidence in policy formation and implementation.*

67 G. Bonnet, Immigration NZ using data system to predict likely troublemakers, *Radio New Zealand* [website], Wellington, 2018, www.radionz.co.nz/news/national/354135/immigration-nz-using-data-system-to-predict-likely-troublemakers, accessed 30 April 2018.

68 Note the Lancet retraction in 2010 twelve years after an article criticising the MMR vaccine seriously damaging global confidence in the vaccine.

69 J. Doogue, *Reserved Judgment of Chief Judge Jan-Marie Doogue in WorkSafe New Zealand v Ministry of Social Development,* District High Court, Wellington, CRI-2015-085-002309, [2016] NZDC 12806, 2016.

70 A. Isaac & B. Ruitenberg, *Air Traffic Control: Human Performance Factors,* Routedge, New York, 2016.

71 Human Rights Commission, Commission asks Kiwis to demand independent inquiry into the abuse of New Zealanders in state care, *Human Rights Commission* [website], 13 February 2017, www.hrc.co.nz/news/commission-asks-kiwis-demand-independent-inquiry-abuse-new-zealanders-state-care/, accessed 30 April 2018.

72 Supreme Court of New Zealand, Anna Elizabeth Osborne and Sonya Lynne Rockhouse v Worksafe New Zealand and The District Court at Wellington, *Supreme Court of New Zealand* [website], 23 November 2017, www.courtsofnz.govt.nz/cases/anna-elizabeth-osborne-and-sonya-lynne-rockhouse-v-worksafe-new-zealand/@@images/fileMediaNotes?r=881.38609417, accessed 30 April 2018.

73 The severity of response generated by an administrative process needs to be accompanied by the appropriate certainty of guilt. After two Court cases to evict tenants were dismissed, Housing New Zealand has admitted that their test to measure the presence of methamphetamine is not fit for purpose. See B. Collins, 'Housing NZ ignored warnings over meth evictions', *Radio New Zealand* [website],

28 October 2106, www.radionz.co.nz/news/political/316591/housing-nz-ignored-warnings-over-meth-evictions, accessed 30 April 2018.

74 Ministry of Health, 'Health targets: Increased immunisation', *Ministry of Health* [website], 18 November 2016, www.health.govt.nz/new-zealand-health-system/health-targets/about-health-targets/health-targets-increased-immunisation, accessed 30 April 2018.

75 Keeping alive the Kaimanawa horses versus protecting the plateau fauna is an example of this sort of tension. See Department of Conservation, 'Kaimanawa Wild Horses Plan', *Department of Conservation,* 2006, www.doc.govt.nz/about-us/science-publications/conservation-publications/threats-and-impacts/animal-pests/kaimanawa-wild-horses-plan/, accessed 30 April 2018.

76 Social Policy Evaluation and Research Unit, *Evaluation of the Family Violence Integrated Safety Response Pilot: Final Report,* Social Policy Evaluation and Research Unit, Wellington, 2017.

77 Even here, governments actions can impose further costs on citizens, as occurred with the South Canterbury Finance: F. O'Sullivan, 'Fran O'Sullivan: Doing it on the cheap a false economy', *New Zealand Herald* [website], 8 April 2016, www.nzherald.co.nz/business/news/article.cfm?c_id=3&objectid=10718035, accessed 30 April 2018.

78 A. Isaac, 'The Cave Creek incident: A reasoned explanation', *Australasian Journal of Disaster and Trauma Studies,* no. 3, 1997, pp. 1-15.

79 Radio New Zealand, 'Farmers reject Greens' farming-pollution policy', *Radio New Zealand* [website], 2 September 2017, www.radionz.co.nz/news/election-2017/338567/farmers-reject-greens-farming-pollution-policy, accessed 30 April 2018.

80 D. Fisher, 'GCSB found to have illegally spied on others in new Megaupload twist', *New Zealand Herald* [website], 25 August 2017, www.nzherald.co.nz/nz/news/article.cfm?c_id=1&objectid=11911084, accessed 30 April 2108.

81 If you have unpaid fines for traffic offences the Ministry of Justice can issue Driver licence stop orders which suspend your licence (or disqualify you if you don't have a current licence) until you pay the fines or come to an arrangement with the courts for repayment. It's a criminal offence to drive while a drive licence stop order is in force against you. You can be jailed for up to three months or fined up to $4,500, and you'll also get an additional disqualification for at least six months. For an overview of driving and traffic law see: Driving and traffic law: Community Law, 'What this chapter covers', *Community Law* [website]. n.d., communitylaw.org.nz/community-law-manual/chapter-33-driving-and-traffic-law/what-this-chapter-covers-chapter-33/, accessed 30 April 2108.

82 Social Security (Stopping Benefit Payments for Offenders Who Repeatedly Fail to Comply with Community Sentences) Amendment Bill.

83 S. Denny et al., *Health Services in New Zealand Secondary Schools and the Associated Health Outcomes for Students,* University of Auckland, Auckland, 2014.

84 The Catholic Church claims data showed that the gap between first alleged incident of child sexual abuse and the date when the claim was received by the Catholic Church authority was more than 30 years in 59 per cent of the claims, and more than 20 years in 81 per cent of claims. The average time between the first alleged incident date and the date the claim was received was 33 years (Royal Commission into Institutional Responses to Child Sexual Abuse, *Final Report: Volume 2 Nature and Cause,* Attorney-Generals' Department, ACT, 2017, p. 68).

85 M. Tran, 'Government drug advisor David Nutt sacked, *The Guardian* [website], 30 October 2009, www.theguardian.com/politics/2009/oct/30/drugs-adviser-david-nutt-sacked, accessed 30 April 2018.

86 Three strikes and you're out law (section 86 of the Sentencing Act 2002). This led to a case where an inmate received seven additional years for pinching prison officers bottom described in M. Mather, 'Seven years' jail for prison bum grab', *Stuff* [website], 24 November 2016, www.stuff.co.nz/national/crime/86818649/seven-years-jail-for-prison-bum-grab, accessed 30 April 2018.

87 New Zealand Productivity Commission, *More Effective Social Services.*

88 Family Violence Death Review Committee, *Family Violence Death Review Committee Fifth Annual Report.*

89 Statistics New Zealand, 'Voter turnout', *Statistics New Zealand* [website], n.d., archive.stats.govt.nz/browse_for_stats/snapshots-of-nz/nz-social-indicators/Home/Trust%20and%20participation%20in%20government/voter-turnout.aspx#info13, accessed 30 April 2018.

90 R. Macfie, 'South Dunedin's flood fiasco', *Noted* [website], 21 June 2016, www.noted.co.nz/currently/social-issues/south-dunedins-flood-fiasco, accessed 30 April 2018.

91 O'Neill, 'Holding Accountability to Account'.

About the authors

Len Cook has had an extensive career in official statistics as New Zealand's Government Statistician from 1992 to 2000 and then National Statistician of the United Kingdom until 2005. Until recently he was Chair of the Board of the Social Policy Research and Evaluation Unit, and is currently a member of the Remuneration Authority.

He is a regular contributor on matters of public administration, official statistics and population related issues.

This wide-ranging experience has equipped Len well to engage in the challenge of the information age as it affects all aspects of public administration, from political life, public sector leadership, the place of science in government and the relationship of the State with its citizens.

Robert Hughes has more than 25 years of experience as a strategic management consultant. He is principal of the consulting firm Hughes Consulting Limited and former partner in the multinational business advisory firm KPMG. Hughes Consulting counsel significant organisations in the private and public sectors. Robert holds a Doctorate and professional credentials as a: Management Consultant, Information Technology Professional, Engineer, and Manager.

Robert brings experience in information, communications, logistics and infrastructure networks which contribute to, and in turn are affected by the digital economy. The State has an important role in shaping these interactions and their consequences for its citizens.